SHINE
IT UP

Jackie Gillies

SHINE
IT UP

THE INSPIRATIONAL TRUE STORY

hachette
AUSTRALIA

hachette
AUSTRALIA

Published in Australia and New Zealand in 2019
by Hachette Australia
(an imprint of Hachette Australia Pty Limited)
Level 17, 207 Kent Street, Sydney NSW 2000
www.hachette.com.au

10 9 8 7 6 5 4 3 2 1

 A catalogue record for this
book is available from the
National Library of Australia

ISBN: 978 0 7336 4214 2 (paperback)

Cover design by Christabella Designs
Cover photograph courtesy of John Tsiavis
Typeset in Sabon LT Std by Kirby Jones
Printed and bound in Australia by McPherson's Printing Group

 The paper this book is printed on is certified against the
Forest Stewardship Council® Standards. McPherson's Printing Group
holds FSC® chain of custody certification SA-COC-005379. FSC®
promotes environmentally responsible, socially beneficial and
economically viable management of the world's forests.

To the love of my life, Ben

Contents

Introduction

If you've seen me on television, you know I like to encourage people to 'shine, shine, shine' or 'shine it up'. When I was in my late teens I started saying 'shine it up' as a way of blessing other people. It made sense. If we can all wish each other the best – and mean it – the world is a nicer place to live in. And wouldn't you want someone to do that for you? I know I do!

But I know things aren't always shiny, or easy. Life can be hard and throw up many challenges. I lost my way and sense of self and I stopped saying 'shine it up' for a while. For years. There were reasons, and they were hard to get past. But I kept trying to work it out, to figure out what my path in life was. I had to admit I'd been struggling and do something about it. That's when I started saying 'shine' again. Wherever I was working at the time, if people walked in, I'd say, 'You've got to shine it up. You've got to shine, shine, shine.' I was giving them a message but also reminding myself that what you put out into the universe comes back.

All the time, it was almost like my guardian angels and the universe were saying to me, 'Bless other people with shine and it will come back to you.' I listened to what I was being told. My angels have been with me always. I believe everyone has them. And I believe everyone can shine it up. It takes courage to follow the path the universe shows you to take – especially when it is outside the norm. But I can tell you, when I did, my life changed for the better.

I'm getting ahead of myself, though, because you don't know why I had all those years of not being able to tell anyone to shine it up – especially myself – yet. You also don't know how I came to have a life where I feel so blessed and grateful to be surrounded by love. That's all ahead of us, in this book. This is my story, but it can also empower yours. We all have difficulties in life and sometimes it feels impossible to get past them. But we can – and the good news is that you're not on your own. There's more support in this world and in the universe than you can imagine. Strength of spirit and resilience can be developed and you can rewrite your own story.

So, if you're at a point in your life where there's no shine, come along with me and find out how you can get that back. And if your life has plenty of shine, you're welcome too – there's plenty of moments in this book that I hope will make you laugh or connect to, and maybe you'll see a bit of yourself in them.

It all comes down to one thing:

Are you ready to shine it up?

An Aussie childhood – with angels

I grew up in Australia but I'm from a European family – a Croatian family. I grew up with my mum, Svetlana, and dad, Ivan, two brothers, Bobby and Milan, and a sister, Angela, in the city of Newcastle in New South Wales.

Because we're European we'd go to other people's houses for dinners and lunches on a Friday night or a Saturday. The strongest memory from my childhood is of something that took place at one of these big gatherings, when I was about five years old.

I remember sitting outside with some of the kids when all of a sudden I saw something I'd never seen before: three little coloured ponies – a bit like My Little Ponies, if you know what those are – flying in front of me. And I saw stars around these ponies. It didn't feel strange, it just felt comfortable. It felt like a loving presence. In hindsight, angels are the only things I can imagine them being. They weren't bad – I knew that. I knew they were good, so what else but angels? I thought the other kids saw them too but when I asked I found out it was just me.

I remember looking through the window where my parents and the other adults were sitting, eating and drinking. And there was I, looking at ponies with stars around them, listening to them talking to me. I wasn't frightened. I had the strongest feeling that there was magic in the world and they were part of that magic. It wasn't somebody telling me – I felt it: *This is real, this is not made up.* I knew I had to remember the moment. *This is magic. This is something more.* As I got older I would think about that day, wondering, *Was that even real?* But I know that it was real and they were angels. Showing me ponies instead of some big person standing in front of me – giving me something my five-year-old mind could relate to – was their way of making me feel safe rather than scared. I don't understand how that works, by the way – I just know it's true. I'm sure there are things you don't completely understand that you know are true too. That you *feel*. We talk ourselves out of a lot of these gut feelings, but we shouldn't.

The timing of seeing these angels was significant: I was about to start going to school, and while I had just been made aware of magic, it's almost as if I stopped allowing it in because I knew I was about to encounter people who didn't see the world the same way. The other kids I was with hadn't seen them – so already I felt different. Difference isn't easy when you're young. I believe the angels knew that was going to happen so they were giving me advice: *We're going to show you this and we're going to make you remember this when it's the right time because we know you're going to follow a path. You're going to forget about the angels for a minute because you're going to start living your everyday life with other kids and forgetting the magic of angels and intuition.* But they were also telling me that even if I forgot about them, they would be there waiting – they would *always* be there.

When I look back, I realise that I often used to play with spirits and I thought that was normal, but I cut it off, like most human beings do. You probably did this too. I bet when you were a child you played with imaginary friends and you knew – fundamentally knew – that the world was so much more than what you could see. Who do you think those imaginary friends were if they weren't spirits or your angels? Those who have passed over are with us all the time, whether we can see them or not.

When we start going to school, though, we're growing up and coming into responsibilities – and life is becoming more regimented: you have to go to school and do homework and listen to your parents and teachers, so you put that other less demanding part of your existence to the side.

Spirits are always there, though. They never leave. We human beings wonder why we go through all this turmoil in our lives; I think it's because we forget about spirits, and about the power of the spirit within us. The power of our intuition. It is so important to *listen* to your intuition. People stop listening around the time they start going to school – and that's what happened to me.

* * *

My mother once told me, 'When you were born, your father wasn't allowed to see you for three days.' This was in Yugoslavia, as it was then, and the rule was that fathers couldn't visit newborns for three days. I was born in the part of Yugoslavia that is now Croatia. My father is Croatian and my mother is Serbian, but they met in Australia. I'll tell you more about that later on.

When I was born, my dad had a bottle of scotch – to celebrate – and he was sitting at the hospital saying,

'My daughter's been born, I've got my bottle of scotch, I want to go in and see my daughter.'

They said, 'You can't go in yet.'

He said, 'I don't want to wait any more!' My father is not shy about saying what he wants.

So they let him in.

Mum described the moment to me: 'When your father held you, I saw a golden light shoot through and around your dad, and around you. I know this sounds crazy, but I saw it.' She said she had never seen anything like it in her life, except for one day when she had a dream, before my older brother, Bobby, was born. She dreamt that she was saying, 'If there's a God, you need to keep my faith in my children,' and she saw a golden light and a face, and she believed it was the face of God. God said to her, 'Two more days and you'll get your results.' Two days after that she found out she was having my brother, and everything she'd prayed for came to fruition.

Of my birth, Mum said, 'When your dad held you, that was an experience that nobody would believe unless they were there.' The light that connected me and Dad has bound us together always. He always was, and still is, a very strong, confident protector.

My early years were spent running around after my brother and eventually becoming a big sister when

Angela was born. She was in the pram Mum was pushing the first day I went to school in Speers Point. I remember holding onto the pram as we walked into the school yard for me to begin Kindergarten. I looked at the other kids and thought, *I don't want to be here.*

I remember my mum's hands and her fingernails and the polish on them as she held onto the pram. There was a girl who lived behind us who went to the same school; she came over and said, 'It's okay.' I put my hand out to take hers, but I really didn't want to be there. I did not want to go into that classroom, I did not want to be going to school.

It's not that I was a nervous kid; I was always quite confident. When I was four we lived in New Lambton – a different part of Newcastle – and there was a school behind us. Mum said I used to slip out the back of our house with my pyjamas on, run in to the school and sit in the classroom and say, 'I'm here.' I'd talk to the kids and the teachers would allow me to stay. Not that I remember doing that.

By the time we moved to Speers Point, though, and I was facing Kindergarten, I didn't want to go to school anymore.

I soon found out why: I was made to feel like an outsider because I wasn't born in Australia. The teacher said, 'You'll all sit in rows of where you were born,' and everybody would be in their Newcastle Hospital row and I'd be in a row by myself with everybody looking at me. It didn't happen just the once, either, so it was almost as if I was being singled out. 'Jackie, you're from *Yu-go-slaav-ia*,' she said. I used to get embarrassed by that.

I was always getting into trouble for talking – except I wasn't talking to other kids, because I was sitting on my own. That didn't stop the teacher blaming me for other kids talking. 'Jackie, you talk too much,' she said. 'Jackie, stop talking.'

It's probably no surprise that some of the other kids thought I'd make a good target for bullying, and there was a fair bit of it – but I knew how to stand up and give it back. I didn't punch anyone or anything like that. It was more that my confidence hadn't left me; it was almost as if I knew I was going to be bullied so I was prepared to stand up for myself. I accepted I was from a different country and my last name was weird. I was Jakica Ivancevic, not Jackie Smith or Jackie Jones, and I was in a very Anglo-Saxon school. Being bullied was horrible.

Being in that class was the start of realising I was different. I wasn't Australian but I *was* Australian: I left Yugoslavia when I was one month old. I spoke perfect

English, my mum spoke English, my dad spoke English. My parents never segregated our family. We had Australian friends because my dad worked in the mines and made friends there.

When I think about it now, I realise I had some racist teachers and I wish I could go back now and tell them so. Or maybe tell them off for being racist. Their behaviour and attitudes told the other kids what was acceptable, so the kids treated me differently too. Even the parents of the other children could be racist; they'd say things like, 'She's got the last name Ivancevic, that doesn't sound normal. You don't need to play with her.'

My older brother's name is Božo, pronounced *Bor-sho*. The English version of his name is Bobby. But that didn't stop some teachers getting on the school loudspeaker system and calling 'Bozo' – pronounced as it was spelled – to the office, even though 'Bobby' was written beside it. Or they couldn't say our last name. One day when I was in high school I said, 'Can you pronounce Smith? Then you can pronounce my last name. Thanks.'

Bobby was awfully bullied, to the extent that he had his head flushed in a toilet at school. He used to run home every day after high school to get away from the kids who were doing that to him. Kids can be cruel, but something inside me gave me strength. No matter what the kids or the teachers did to me, I wasn't going to play the victim. Rocks used to be thrown at me when I walked across the quadrangle and they'd yell out things to me. They'd say, 'You wog, go back to your own country!' and 'Get back to yer boat.'

Some people say, 'I was so bullied at school and now I'm depressed.' I understand how a person's spirit can be beaten down and how those scars can come to define a person and their thoughts of themselves. I managed to turn it around. I told myself sometimes that's just life – as tough as that might sound, it's the truth. You have to deal with that stuff and not allow it to diminish your spirit. I was really quite severely bullied but I didn't allow that to make me into a person who is aggressive towards other people. I didn't allow it to define me. What defines me is being inspired by my past and what I've overcome. To know my strength and to embrace my resilience.

Life can be hard, I'm not going to say it's not. We're all going to have trials and tribulations, we're going to have ebbs and flows. Some people have huge trauma to deal with. The thing to remember is, the more you worry about a problem, the bigger it will become and the harder it is to make it go away. But there will always be a day when it will be resolved. I still worry about things, but I talk myself through it and ask myself why would I worry about a situation I can't control? In our society, it's human nature to fear the things we can't control but we should never forget we can control how much we worry about them.

Here's the thing I've learnt: you can buckle under the bullying or you can realise that you've just got to get on with things. My dad was always very good at telling us to stand up for ourselves and what we believed in: 'Don't let anybody put it over you.' Dad came to Australia at a young age and at that time all the Europeans would stick together. Not Dad: he learnt the English language because he loves Australia. He was the only one out of all the Europeans he knew who mixed with Australians and immersed himself in the Australian culture. He not only learnt to speak English but to read and write it, even though he left school when he was still in primary school.

Not that he left all of his European traditional ways behind. My dad was very strict; my mother less so. When I was a kid, Dad did not want us going on sleepovers to our friends' houses. He didn't trust people he didn't know. I didn't go to parties until I was sixteen or so. Ours was a very strict, very European household where my friends had to come to my house – I wasn't allowed to go to theirs. If I had a party they could come to my house but I was rarely allowed to have sleepovers or allowed to go and visit my friends' houses. And all the members of my family had to sit around the table and eat dinner together, which would be a pain sometimes but it meant we were all communicating with each other.

My dad very much wanted his daughters cooking and cleaning – not that I would be at home cooking all the time, but he would say, 'You will clean the house this Saturday,' and I couldn't disobey. I couldn't go out and play until the house was cleaned or I'd done my chores in his vegetable garden. So I didn't always invite my friends over, but when I did they loved coming because there'd be all this food! My dad would say, 'Come on, kids, eat some food, eat up, that's not enough!'

While my father was very strict, he also had (and still has) the biggest heart of gold – he would give you the shirt off his back. He used to invite homeless people to our house on Sunday, and Mum would cook them roast dinners. He was generous with his time and his home, and still is.

When we arrived from Yugoslavia, Dad went to work for Comsteel, then he worked in Sydney, for a mining company, and my mum had to look after us. She didn't have a car, and understandably she didn't want to get on a bus for two hours to go somewhere with three kids under the age of five. So my childhood world was very much school and home and our immediate neighbourhood; I didn't have much of a sense of the rest of Newcastle. I wasn't out in parts of Newie with my friends. Though I did have my next-door neighbours, who were Australian. We always hung out and would go bike riding and climb trees, all the usual childhood stuff, but we never ventured far from home.

However, the part of Newcastle that was mine felt safe – if I walked down to the shops, everybody was always very nice, and the shopkeepers would say hello. I remember going to the shops by myself, or with my brother and sister, and we'd be selling vegetables from my dad's garden out of a little basket – cucumbers for 20 cents and tomatoes – to the neighbours. We used to do really well and we were allowed to keep that money. We certainly didn't lack for activities.

* * *

When I was about four, my cheeky brother Bobby woke me, grabbed my hand and off we went for a walk. He was about five and a half or six years of age. It was something like four o'clock in the morning, but we went over to the park – because we wanted to play. My mother woke up and found we weren't in the house. She freaked out, understandably, and woke up Dad, who also freaked out.

While we were in the park I remember wanting to go down the slippery dip, so my brother was helping me up the rungs of the ladder. I honestly believe my angels were protecting Bobby and me that night because I remember people walking around the park at that time – and they weren't out for a jog. I was too young to know what they were really up to but it was probably not legal.

The next thing I remember is thinking, *This is amazing*, because I was in a cop car and I put the cop's hat on my head. I was such a cute young kid, let me tell you – I had chubby cheeks, curly hair. When we got home there was Dad in his undies and his singlet, screaming, and all I said was, 'Hi, Daddy.' My brother got smacked so hard in front of the coppers, and I remember my dad saying, 'I'll give you "Hi, Daddy".'

I don't think my brother was allowed out of his room for the whole next day, because he scared our parents so much. But Bobby used to do things like that all the time. He even jumped out of a high window, landed on his bum and winded himself. He used to do dumb things because he thought they looked fun.

* * *

When my parents moved to Speers Point, our house was the oldest in the street. It was very modest. It was a classic weatherboard worker's cottage with a tin roof and it needed a lot of work. It looked like a shack. It was always clean and tidy but it was really small.

My parents were so proud of their home but I was embarrassed because some kids from school weren't that keen on it. 'Look at your house,' they'd say, 'it's so old, it's so disgusting.' It's amazing how early in life people start being judgemental, and it's not fun being on the receiving end of that judgement. I wasn't used to it because neither of my parents are judgemental; the first time I encountered it was when I went to school.

I'd like to say that in response to the bullying about the house I was always like my mum, who is very calm and collected, but sometimes I took after my dad instead and I would give back as good as I got to those kids. If someone said, 'You're just a wog,' I'd answer: 'What did you say?' By the end of primary school I'd become really great at standing up for myself. I remember being in Year Seven and someone saying to me, 'Get back on your boat.' I turned around and said, 'Take your shackles off, you convict.' He just looked at me. And he never said anything like that to me again. I went home and cried about it, but I didn't let him keep me down. I dusted myself off. I really do thank my parents for instilling a sense of confidence in me that helped build resilience.

I loved my family childhood experiences, even if other kids would try and make me feel ashamed of it.

There were a lot of trees and greenery at that house – our garden was full of flowers and vegetables. Dad wanted his kids to learn how to do the garden and do all the house duties, like washing dishes and vacuuming the floors and cleaning the bathroom, before we could go out and play. I had to get out in the garden and dig up weeds and my sister and I would clean that house with music playing to keep us company. Meanwhile, we knew that the three kids who lived next door would be waiting for us to finish so we could all hang out. We spent time with them every day. Between our house and theirs was an empty block, and each time Angela and I finished the cleaning we would yell out 'cooee' across the block so the neighbours would know we were ready.

The neighbour kids actually loved helping out when we worked in the garden, but I just thought, *Who else does this in Australia? Is there anybody else who has to do the garden?* And, yes, there were: most of the Europeans I knew had parents making them do the same thing. From a young age I knew how to tell the parsley from the carrots from the tomatoes, so, as Dad said,

'When you grow up you know what it looks like to plant a tomato – this is really good for you.' Food was a big thing in our home. And it was cooked in our kitchen and heavily influenced by my mother and father's heritage. I didn't know what a meat pie looked like until I went to a birthday party because we'd never eaten one. I was seventeen and a half when I tried McDonald's for the first time. The only junk food we were allowed was if, say, a visitor came over – and in our culture they would bring a case of beer for the adults and a bag of lollies for all the kids. So as soon as we'd get those we'd scoff, scoff, scoff. We weren't allowed soft drinks either, only cordial on rare occasions.

Sometimes our visitors were our non-Croatian neighbours, who would come over and eat the Croatian food that my mum would make. Mum and Dad would say, 'Stay for dinner,' or for lunch, whatever it was. There were always big pots of food, and for me that was normal – although some might say it was overeating! But if you came to my house there'd be a big bowl of salad, a big bowl of potatoes and pumpkin, another bowl of vegetables and a jug of gravy, then you'd have a soup before you ate the main meal. And every Sunday we had a roast dinner with soup – and that was after bacon and eggs in the morning. Then there were the cakes my mum would make – amazing Croatian cakes that our neighbours, in particular, loved.

As I look back, I believe that my dad wanted us to learn how to grow plants in the event something ever happened to this world. He would say, 'If there is a bomb –' because there have been many wars in Europe, '– I'm going to tell you now, a lot of your friends wouldn't even know how to grow food. You need to be prepared in the event of everything, anything that happens, any event that means food becomes scarce.' He knew what that felt like. He grew up in an environment where food was scarce and he needed to work for it; later, after he moved to Australia, there was a war going on in his homeland. He'd tell us that we didn't know when a war was going to happen, and if it happened in Australia he wanted us to be able to fend for ourselves.

We often don't realise how good we've got it, and I didn't. So many of my friends have said to me since then that they used to love coming to our house, 'because your parents would be there and you'd all have to eat together. You could tell your parents loved each other. It was so connected, and our families didn't have that.' Although sometimes I'd get embarrassed when my friends were there because, when it was hot, my dad would walk around in his singlet, shorts and thongs, and Mum would cook and we'd eat outside – it was just like Dad was still in the village in Croatia. We'd sit under a gum tree, where Dad had set up this 44-gallon drum with a hotplate on top of it. There was a swing we'd all go on and people would walk past. From the street you could see what we were doing: sitting under the tree with five pots on the table, eating, and Dad would have the Rakija out – that's a traditional homemade Croatian spirit – and he'd invite the neighbours over and people would just sit around eating and drinking. I think because my dad grew up with very little food, any person who comes to our house will find food on the table. Even as an adult, if I didn't get up within five minutes of someone arriving to organise coffees and prosciutto and cheese and salamis and breads and olives and gherkins, I'd get a look from Dad.

I saw a difference when I'd go to my friends' homes, though, where my food would be plated up for me. I never understood that – in fact, I didn't like it. I liked the community that comes with sitting and serving as a group. I still do.

* * *

My parents were godparents to a young girl (whose mother has since passed on, God bless her soul) who lived in New Lambton, and my sister and I often stayed at her house, which was next to our own when we still lived there. The girl was my sister's age, so we would always play together; I'm three and a half years older than Angela, but I didn't ever mind playing with the younger kids.

From the age of six, when we visited, my sister and I would stay in a certain room. It was always very, very cold, and I never liked to go into that room. *Ever.* I knew there was a spirit in there. I used to say, 'Uncle Barry and Aunt Rita, can I sleep on the lounge please?' And I was told, 'There's not enough room, just go up into bed.'

One night when I was thirteen, Angela and I woke up to the sound of a dog barking. I didn't want to look out from under the covers, so we hid under the covers, crying, when we heard someone singing, 'Ring a ring a rosy, a pocket full of posy.' We looked out and there were kids' spirits in front of my sister and me, singing and holding hands, and a dog right there in front of the bed, barking.

Angela and I were bawling our eyes out. We flew back under the covers and in my head I began telling the spirits to get out of there. But they wouldn't go, and we kept crying until finally Uncle Barry turned the lights on, and I told him what had happened. He said, 'I know there are spirits in here because it's always cold.'

I told my mum the next day and said that I'd never stay in that house again. After that, when we did visit it would be during the day and I would run past that room.

There's an epilogue to that story, as told to me by my mum long after we stopped having sleepovers at Aunty Rita's. One day Mum was peeling potatoes while Dad was outside working. Through the window she could see the side of Rita and Barry's house; there were three windows. Rita and Barry and their kids were away on a holiday, but as Mum looked out she saw a woman with long black hair inside the house, walking past the windows. Mum looked again, thinking it was just her eyes playing up. She kept peeling the potatoes. She saw the woman walk past again but the woman didn't look at her.

Mum called out to Dad and said, 'There's somebody in Rita and Barry's house.' Dad said, 'Don't be so stupid.' But Dad heard somebody in the house and saw them walk past the windows too. My parents rang the police, who turned up a bit later with torches and they went looking through the windows of the house because there should not have been anybody there.

There *was* something in that house, all right – and it never left. I know this because I have always seen spirits, even if I used to think they were in my imagination. It was *never* my imagination. *I have seen them.* So it makes sense that my mum saw the spirit there. She still made us sleep in that house after knowing it was haunted! I have said to my mum, 'You tortured me by letting me stay in that house.'

After that experience with the spirits, Barry did some research into the history of the house and found that the land had been lived on by convicts when they first came to Australia. I believe the spirits knew that I could see them. And after that one incident of 'Ring a ring a rosy', I never saw them again.

* * *

Dad used to study martial arts when he lived in Melbourne and he made it right up to just about getting his black tip, but that's when he moved to Newcastle. Which was why, one day, he said to Bobby and me, 'All right, you two are going to karate.'

'I don't want to go to karate!' I said. I was doing dance lessons and I loved those.

But Dad said, 'You're going to karate, both of you. Off you go.'

Bobby didn't like karate so he'd say he was going and then he'd just sit under the house. I think he was being bullied at karate by the kids, because of his name – they'd call him Bozo the Clown. But I said, 'Come on, Bobby we're going,' and he'd occasionally join me.

There was a tree on the way to karate that we used to climb up. I was never afraid – I was a tomboy, I used to climb up very high trees and swing from one branch to another. I wasn't afraid of heights. One day we climbed the tree and before I started swinging I heard a warning in my head: *Do not swing onto the next branch.* I thought it was my own voice, so I swung over anyway, and fell and landed on my arm. When I stood up, the bone was sticking up a bit, so I was fairly sure I'd done something serious to it. It also hurt quite a bit, so that was another clue.

We went home and I said, 'Mum, my arm is so sore,' and she didn't realise how bad it was, because she had three kids to worry about. Dad was away working, so she probably wondered what she should do: *Should I take her to hospital now, do I pack up all the kids, do you think this will keep just another couple of hours until I can get somebody over here?* But I was so glad when she just wrapped me up and put us all in the car and off we went to the hospital.

She was told I had a greenstick fracture and needed to have an operation. Mum cried because this had never happened to anyone in the family and, of course, the doctors had to say there was a risk I could die because of the general anaesthetic. She couldn't talk to Dad about it, because he was away. Meanwhile, I was wondering what all the fuss was about.

I remember the mask coming down and I was talking to a spirit, saying, 'I am not going to go under with this mask,' even as I'm looking down at the needle that's in my sore hand. So the doctor was saying, 'Count back from five,' and I'm thinking, *I'm not going anywhere.*

Four.

I was still fighting it.

Then, *bang*, it all went black, and the next minute they're wheeling me out and I was okay. But the point of the story is that I remember something in my head saying, *Do not jump, do not go to that next branch*, and I ignored it and broke my arm. It was a very early, very painful lesson in trusting my intuition.

My Croatian family

My parents met over grapes. Dad knew my mother in the way Europeans did then: Dad was in Melbourne and Mum was living in Melbourne and, you know, the Europeans get together and eat and have dances and all those types of things. The way Mum tells it, they were at a friend's house – Mum was staying at this house with her mother, because they were waiting on a flat they were hoping to rent. My mother and grandmother had moved to Australia from Serbia years earlier when Mum was ten years old, after my grandmother had divorced Mum's father. That fateful day grapes were brought out and Mum went to take one, and the son of the lady who owned the house said, 'She can't eat those grapes, we bought them.' And my dad, who's older than Mum, turned around and said, 'If she wants to eat those grapes, she'll eat them. Because I bought them.' My dad came from a very poor village and, as I've mentioned, one thing he doesn't like is when there's not enough food on the table. He always wants to see people eat because it makes him feel happy.

Mum said, 'I just knew as soon as I saw your father that he was the one.' She fell in love with his eyes, and she fell in love with his personality. My mother ended up running off to Sydney with my father – it turned out he felt the same way. They were in love.

They got married and had Bobby. Then they took a holiday in Croatia and Mum fell pregnant with me. After returning to Australia they made plans to move back to Croatia, so Bobby and Dad and pregnant Mum went back. My dad bought a block of land and they started to look at building on it, but not long after I was born Dad was down to his last thousand dollars and he said to Mum, 'If we don't leave now, we're never getting out of here.' They had to wait for my visa to come through, because I wasn't born in Australia, so Dad left me and my mother and went to Australia with Bobby. The embassy told Mum, 'You can come to Australia but Jackie can't.' So we had to stay and get all the paperwork sorted. She wasn't going to leave her daughter behind.

It took a while but the family was soon reunited and we all settled into life in Australia, with no plans to leave. Dad wanted to make a good life here. My dad's real, and he is the most generous person you will ever meet. There have been times when people have knocked on my parents' door in the early hours of the morning – people coming through from Sydney, Europeans or Aussies, or whoever worked with Dad – and my mum would get up and cook them bacon and eggs. That was just the norm, that was what she did because my dad is always very generous with people and food and money, and my mum is very kind-hearted and supportive. Dad doesn't want to see people unhappy – or not fed enough!

In those first years, Dad always had to battle because he was Croatian and his English wasn't great when he first came to Australia, but he is very good at making friends and is very funny. Once they get to know him people love and accept my dad because of his loyalty and because of the person he is.

I'm quite like my father: I'm very loud and very confident. Not that my mum isn't confident too – let me tell you, she wears the pants in the family – it's just that she's very quiet about it. But when she speaks up, everyone listens.

Around the house my dad yells because that's his character. Our neighbours would often hear Dad yelling, 'Jackie! Bobby! Get home! Time for dinner!' Most people might think he was gruff and wonder if he was being abusive, but yelling is just what he does. He is loud.

Just as his voice is big, so is his heart. Dad worked really hard and sent money overseas to his family. Granted, he earned good money working in the mines, but after paying bills, supporting us, living in Sydney and paying the mortgage and sending money overseas, it only left so much.

We always had a roof over our heads, though, and we always had food and all the necessities, and we were raised really well; we would never know if there wasn't enough of anything in the house. Maybe there were times when money was tight but Bobby and I would never know about it. If there was just a sausage in the fridge and somebody came over, Dad would offer the sausage, and then he'd pull out some Rakija, or whatever he had. Dad's generous spirit never dimmed. He'd give you his last dollar or the shirt off his back. And Mum supported him every step of the way.

I mentioned earlier that I am a lot like my father. And there is another aspect to that. My dad is very, very psychic. He sees things the way I do; he doesn't tell me, but I know he does. He knew when his mother passed and when his father passed; he knew when they were sick. (The only times I saw them I was a baby.) He'd know when a friend or relative was dying. He'd see them and he'd just know that they'd passed. Then he'd receive a telegram the next day from Croatia saying he needed to come because there was going to be a funeral.

I've only met my maternal grandmother once, because she moved back to Serbia – and because she disowned my mother when Mum married my dad, because Dad was Croatian. Mum didn't see her father for many, many years after her mother divorced him, but they are still in touch now, and she has half-sisters, and she is in contact with them too.

My mum and dad really are soulmates. Their relationship is a massive inspiration for me when it comes to loyalty, a quality that is hugely important to me. That's not surprising, given I grew up seeing it lived out every single day.

* * *

For all my parents' generosity, they had some strict rules. As strong-willed as I am, I knew I had to do as they said.

When I was in high school, I wasn't allowed to go to parties until I was over sixteen and, when I finally did, I was driven there and driven home – which is something most parents were doing. But I remember one time I went to a party Dad had said I couldn't go to – and he walked in and collected me. It was so embarrassing, as you can imagine!

When Dad says something, that's it. You can't sway him. If I said, 'Come on, I really want to go out,' and he said, 'No,' then that was the end of that. And I listened. Even at twenty-one, I listened. I didn't start drinking alcohol at parties until I was twenty-four.

My little sister didn't listen to my dad. She was out there. Angela is younger than me but she's not the youngest: my brother Milan was born quite a few years after her; he's in his twenties now. And those two younger ones got away with so much more than Bobby and I did. I think Bobby had to go through the trials and tribulations of being the eldest. He wasn't allowed to do anything. And as the eldest girl I wasn't either, and if I did go out, I'd have to go out with him, which was a pretty European thing to do.

When I was seventeen, after I got my driver's licence, my parents bought me a car – a convertible Ford Capri. I thought I was a movie star: I put the roof up, put music on – some Croatian music, some Aussie music, some R&B – and I was rolling, rolling down into Newie, thinking I was God's gift, as you do. I was high on the independence of not having to always say, 'Dad, I'm doing this, I'm doing that.' But if I got too cocky there were times when Dad took my keys off me to stop me going out.

Even though my sister got away with more, she also used to cop it more than me, because she never listened. We'd go out and when we got home late, our dad would be sitting there in his singlet and undies – because he'd have gotten up out of bed. He'd be snacking on salamis, prosciutto, cheese and bread while he waited for us to return. He'd say, 'It's three o'clock in the morning, I told you to be home by one-thirty.' When I first started going out I was always home by one-thirty. It took two years before I even stretched that. But still he'd be waiting, sitting there eating. My dad's always eating. I eat a lot too. I must get that from him.

So he'd be sitting there, saying, 'Hello, daughter, who was out, what did you do tonight?' He wanted me to tell him everything, and sometimes I think he knew already, because he knew a lot of the Europeans in Newie. 'So how many drinks did you have tonight?'

'I didn't have any,' I'd reply – and usually I didn't, but as I got older there were times when I did start to drink a little bit. Bacardi Breezers, mainly. In our culture at Christmas, and Good Friday and Easter, we had a sip of wine. In Europe by the time we're teenagers we pretty much know what alcohol tastes like. It meant that alcohol wasn't very interesting to me as a teenager, whereas there were a lot of other kids I knew who, by the time they were eighteen, were getting drunk.

Giving sips of wine to a young teenager is just one element of my culture. My family's culture has a massive importance in my life and it really did shape me, especially when it comes to my friends and the people around me. When it comes to relationships, my culture influences who I want to be with and spend time with. As I've said, I'm very big on loyalty, on making sure that what I give out comes back – and if somebody does something damaging to me they're forgiven but I don't let them back in with me – I do not give second chances. If you can't give me what I give you, then I don't have time for you anymore. I know the person I am, and that comes from my heritage. If I can't come to you and tell you the things I'm going through or if I can't ring you up at four o'clock in the morning needing someone to talk to, then you're not my friend. And if I see somebody who lies or is dishonest, well … there have been quite a few times when I have just said to a person's face, 'You're out.'

As I was growing up, we would have all the Europeans we knew come to our house or we'd go to their houses and nobody would ever say anything about Mum being Serbian, even though it could have been contentious with some Croatian people. The war lasted from 1991 to 1995 and resulted in the breaking up of the federation that was known as Yugoslavia. After that time the countries became their own republics: Bosnia and Herzegovina, Serbia, Croatia, Macedonia, Montenegro and Slovenia. We had friends from all of these regions as well as Australian friends and there was never any tension. My dad hung out with lots of different people. He didn't see gender, he didn't see race, he didn't see any of that stuff, he just saw you for who you were. But that's probably why my dad backed away from really political people. He doesn't like talking about politics. I don't talk about politics either, because it causes a lot of disruptions in people's lives – not to mention wars.

Dad was very, very strict about us not talking about the politics of the war. He would say that people who didn't have the history didn't have the right to talk about politics; unless you were there, unless you were in that war, unless you were part of that, or part of a particular issue, you didn't have the right to discuss it. There were – and are – a lot of people who will discuss the Yugoslavian War who weren't even there, and Dad's position was: you weren't up there fighting, you didn't lose your life, you're here in Australia, safe and sound, so why are you sharing your brainwashed mentality in this country? It's a beautiful country and he is very proud to be here. I am too.

My dad is a very proud Aussie. If there were other Australians in the house when Europeans came to visit, he wouldn't speak Croatian. He'd say, in English, 'I'm not speaking our language while we're sitting around the table with other Aussies sitting here, because it's not right.' If some of our visitors couldn't speak a word of English, then he'd translate. He was very respectful of people's time and who people were. And still is.

I believe Dad really misses Croatia and missed his brothers and his sisters. I believe there were times he probably did think, *Have I made the right decision?* But when he looks at his lifestyle and progress, the food and financial security, he always gives thanks to Australia. He says, even now, 'We are so lucky that Australia accepted me and for what Australia gives to people. We are the luckiest country in the world.' Dad has been in other countries so he has a fair idea of how lucky and how blessed we are.

But there have been times, for example at Christmas, when he chokes up, after he speaks to all the relatives.

He'd be drinking some Rakija, speaking to everyone on the phone for three hours, and there'd be a $1700 bill. He didn't care, he just wanted to talk to people he loved and missed. He would wake me up at three in the morning to speak to everybody in Croatia: 'Your aunties are on the phone, your uncles are on the phone, you gotta get on there and you gotta talk to them!' I'd always say, 'I'm tired,' and he'd say, 'Hurry up, Jackie! Hurry up, you gotta speak to them!'

Dad loves all of us equally, of course – but if you ask Bobby, Angela and Milan they'll say I'm definitely his favourite! All my family knows it. Dad always says, 'Okay, number one, what's going on?' However, I think just because you have more in common with one child it doesn't mean you love them more than the next child, it just means you have a different connection with that person because you can communicate better with them. It's like life: you connect with people you can have a deeper conversation with.

* * *

I think I'm Dad's favourite not because I was born in Croatia or because I am the oldest girl but because I listen to him. Angela doesn't, she argues all the time.

Bobby's really chilled. He's like my mum and so is Milan. When I was very young, I was very like my mother. I really started to speak up (like my dad) once I was in my twenties. But I was always very loud, and if my dad said not to do something, I would listen. And I certainly didn't talk back.

As we were growing up, my sister and I argued all the time. We never punched each other but we'd grab each other's hair and pull it. We fought a lot. But we'd never fight in front of Dad. If something didn't go Angela's way she would always scream – I remember that scream! When she was six or seven years old she used to chuck tantrums, and she was very spoilt because she was the youngest for such a long time. I also think she got away with more because she was the youngest. I was the first-born daughter so I was the good girl who listened, whereas she didn't listen to Dad, or even to Mum. But I love my sister and I remember that I always wanted to kiss her cheeks because she had these chubby cheeks; she'd say, 'Get off me!'

I think sometimes my brother and sister thought, *Oh, you're always Dad's number one, get lost.* But I believe Mum favoured the boys more so it evened out. Not that I have definitive proof!

Like me, my mother is psychic: she has dreams that give her information, and she'll acknowledge that but she won't go on about it. Mum said that when my paternal grandfather passed away, Dad was lying on his side next to her, his back turned, and Mum was on her side too, looking at him, when all of a sudden she saw this big white light in the bathroom past my dad, and as she looked at Dad she saw my grandfather looking at her through Dad's back, and he was all bones and then he just crumbled away. The next day there was a telegram to Dad saying, 'You've got to come now, your dad's died.' So Mum knew that that was my grandfather's way of saying, 'I'm here, and I'm now shining off to the heavens.' Mum sees things like that all the time and so does my dad. He admits that he is psychic: he does see, he does feel and he does know.

I feel like my childhood was happy in the sense that I had a family who loved me and I had a family that was very protective of me. They were overprotective, but they did the best that they could with the knowledge they had. That's how I look at it now, that's how I look at my life and what I have. I always give thanks. I had a blessed childhood. Home was always safe. It was outside of our family unit that troubles found me.

The girl most likely to ...

A lot of my problems and insecurities started at school, not at home, because my father and mother always instilled a lot of confidence in all of us. At home was where I learnt so much about people and life. Dad would teach us how to observe people and learn about them. He wanted us to learn when people were being truthful and when they weren't. People would visit and he'd say, 'You can serve some coffees with your mum and you can sit here and watch them, because I want you to learn what life's going to be like.'

He'd say, 'You're going to be among people who don't tell the truth. People lie or they do things because they want to get ahead.' That was a really life-changing thing to hear, and it was true, too.

But at school I had no voice. No child has a voice at school. If you don't agree with something, you don't have the right to say that to the teacher. To say that a primary-school teacher who used to make me sit by myself, seemingly for her own amusement, exploited the fact that I was different by making me *feel* different. If you're different you can be singled out.

I was always confident, though, even at school, and it wasn't confidence born of ego. I still have confidence and I've always been loud; that's never stopped, nor has it recently appeared – it's always been there.

I used to have it in my head that I was going to be known for something. When I was a young girl I would often be daydreaming that I was going to be something big in this world – and when I say 'daydream', I believe I was talking to the universe – I would have this innate feeling that I would be helping people somehow, somewhere. Except I thought it was going to be through dance, because I used to love dancing and singing. I loved being on the stage, I loved performing, and I always thought that this was what I was going to do. From the age of five I used to write on birthday cards, *Love, Famous Jackie*. I don't even know why I did it!

One day at school, a teacher was leaving. The art teacher, Mrs Potter, said to me, 'Jackie, I want you to

go and find all the teachers and get them to sign this.'
It was a card. Obviously, I said yes: I got a free period,
I'm walking around to all the teachers' areas, I thought
it was amazing. I could see everybody signing the card
and writing messages. I decided I'd write on the card
too: I wrote goodbye to whoever it was, *Wish you well,
Love, Famous Jackie*.

And I got my head blown off, even though I was
Mrs Potter's favourite student. I can still hear the call
over the microphone: 'Jackie Ivancevic to the head office
of the art department, please.' I thought Mrs Potter was
going to say, 'Well done.' But she screamed, 'How dare
you write on this card!' So my early instances of being
Famous Jackie weren't always well received ...

You'll notice that I didn't think I was doing anything
wrong there – I wasn't trying to be naughty. I rarely tried
to be naughty. I remember once I was asked if I'd ever
stolen anything and I had: bubblegum, from the corner
shop, when I was seven or eight. Angela was with me
and even though she was much younger she told me to
get packets of bubblegum, so I did. I was her big sister
and should have said no. I remember feeling so damn
guilty about that. I still popped it in my mouth, though.
Those were the days when you could walk down to the
shop without an adult – you could go to the shop with a

note to buy cigarettes for your mum – *Can Jackie please pick up a packet of Benson & Hedges Special Filter times two*, or whatever it was – and then I'd say, 'Can I please have twenty-five cents' worth of lollies?', which always looked like I had five bucks' worth of lollies. I used to love going to the corner shop and getting my milk bottles, my little pineapples and my little red jubes.

One time my brother and I went to church, and Dad gave us some money to put in the tin. Well, we didn't put the money in the tin, we went to the shop and bought Curly Wurlys with it. So maybe I wasn't *always* a good girl, but I tried to be.

The shop wasn't always fun, though. I went down one day to get something for my mum and dad. It was a short walk; everything was tight and close in that neighbourhood. John, the shopkeeper, knew us very well and I was complaining to him, saying, 'I've got to walk home up that hill.' I was about twelve at the time. There was this man standing behind me; I remember a kind of flash when I was speaking, almost like my angels made me look at this man's face, so I turned around.

John's response was, 'Oh, you'll be all right, Jackie, it's only a six-minute walk.'

So I started walking up the street and the man who'd been standing behind me in the shop pulled up in a car beside me. 'How about you jump in my car,' he said, 'and I'll give you a lift to the top?'

I said, 'No, no, I'm not going to do that.' My spirits were talking to me even at that young age, because I had the intuition not to get in that car.

He had this gold car and brown hair and he just looked creepy, and he wouldn't give up. 'Just get in the car and I'll drive you,' he said again, and even though I said no once more, he kept going. 'You're tired, I'll just give you a lift.'

'No,' I said, 'I'm not getting in the car.'

Finally he drove off, but I was freaked out and I stayed near the houses that had Safety House stickers on them. When I got home, I told my dad what had happened. He bolted down to the shop in the car and said to John, 'Where is he?' But poor John didn't know anything.

It was something that I had never heard of happening in my neighbourhood, but I never walked alone like that again. I'm sure this guy wasn't a local. I think that was a moment that could have led me down a different path. Could I have been murdered or kept hidden somewhere? I'll never know, but I'm glad that something in my intuition was screaming out, *You're not getting in that car!*

* * *

I remember in class one time, probably in Year Nine, this guy threw a rubber at me while the teacher had her back turned. She was a history teacher; I always loved history. I was fascinated with Ancient Egypt – Tutankhamun, Nefertiti, all of that stuff – and I'm sure I lived there in a past life. I picked up the rubber and pegged it back at this kid, hard. And he said something like, 'You can suck my dick.' You know how boys that age are. I thought, *You disgusting idiot.* And I said, 'Flop it out, then!' And he flopped it out and I said, 'You sick bastard!'

So there were times when I was bullied but there were times when I would just whip it back. Sometimes I feel guilty saying I was bullied – maybe I was a bully back, but it was in retaliation for being attacked for so long. I would say, 'I'm not going to let you do this!' I remember one guy tried to hit me on the arse and I grabbed his hand, pulling it up and pushing him. I've never been in a fight in my life, but I had the determination that no one was going to stand over me. Maybe this strength also comes from my dad.

There comes a time when a child wants to fight back, or you need to fight back and stand your ground. It doesn't mean that I wanted to hurt anybody, although probably I wanted to inflict the hurt I was receiving back onto that person. Sometimes you have to grow up very quickly, even as a child. You have to handle what life throws at you.

But I didn't always deal with painful things by giving it back to the person who caused it. I believe pain is an energy that can either be toxic, cathartic or rewarding. For me, bullying was a toxic situation because I bottled things up and never talked about them. I'd keep the emotional state caused by the bullying to myself – I wouldn't let anyone know how I felt. Because of this I went through a negative stage: I was never the clever girl, I was never the good-looking chick. I remember this one time I was at home, lying in bed and I felt so tense and like I just didn't want to be there. I may have been fourteen or fifteen. I once even wrapped a leather belt around my neck, just to see what it would feel like. I wasn't what I thought was suicidal; I was just despairing. I just didn't want to be in school. But that's the scary thing: that despair can cause you not to think beyond relief in that moment.

When I was in the first couple of years of high school I remember these boys saying, 'You're so flat the walls are jealous.' I came home, crying, and I said to Mum, 'I've got no boobs,' because I felt so humiliated. The way some boys speak to girls like that *is* humiliating. Many years later Mum told me that she went into her bedroom that day and prayed to God. She said, 'I asked that my daughter would have long legs and big boobs' – because she had prayed for that before I was born. She was teased about being flat-chested and she didn't want that for her daughter. I've got long legs and my boobs started growing at fourteen or fifteen. Out of nowhere. Now I've got E cups and they're all mine. So my Mum's prayers were answered.

Mum told me something else she prayed for was that her first-born child would have blue eyes and blond hair even though we're a dark-haired family. The two things that she prayed for happened, because Bobby has blue eyes and blond hair.

After my boobs started growing, all the guys started paying attention to me but I still retaliated if they were rude. When I was sixteen, seventeen, eighteen, I still felt like I wasn't a good-looking chick, but I knew guys were starting to take notice. I wouldn't give them anything, though. I wouldn't even give them the opportunity. At parties the other kids would have their Bacardi Breezers and other drinks and I'd be walking around with my bottle of water. Guys would try to talk to me and maybe one would try to have a pash but I just wouldn't let it happen, because I had self-respect. I also really give thanks to my dad and mum for the fact that I kept myself to myself in those days – Dad would say things like, 'You keep your pants up' every time I went out, which might sound odd but it's not, it actually made me fully realise that I valued my self-respect a great deal. And I didn't want to be out shagging dudes – although there were so many guys who wanted to be with me precisely because I didn't want to be with them.

My dad would have conversations with me, saying that when a man loves you or really wants you, you'll know it and you'll feel it. He used to speak like that a lot. When I look back, it's almost as though Dad's words sparked something inside me, something that told me, *You own your body, you own what you do with your body, and you must do that with the right intent. Don't just go and sleep with a man because you want attention, don't just go and give yourself away.*

Boys used to call me frigid, and maybe I was, but I chose to be frigid. I used to be angry when they said that, but there was still a part of me that enjoyed being different. I knew one girl who fell pregnant on purpose, just before her fifteenth birthday, in order to keep a man – but he didn't stay with her. It was almost like the angels stuck her in my life to prove that what my dad was saying was right, and that I shouldn't be so angry about what he was saying because there was truth behind it.

But when you're fourteen you don't think about that. There was a time, of course, when I was curious enough to pash a couple of guys, but that was it.

* * *

Dancing and singing were the things that made me happy when I was younger. In primary school I got the lead role as Mary Poppins and was singing 'Chim Chiminey' all around the place. I also used to be part of a dancing troupe that would dance at shows as a performance group. My mother would get on the bus with me three times a week and take me on the forty-minute trip to Newcastle from Speers Point, even when it was raining, to take me to dance classes. I was very committed to it.

I thought dancing and singing was what I was going to do for the rest of my life, and I remember I took open classes at Keane Kids and Brent Street, in Sydney. When I started doing these courses I'd get on the train by myself at two o'clock in the afternoon and arrive in Sydney by four-thirty or five o'clock for the start of the class. My parents were okay with it because they knew I was with two other girls from the Central Coast and after class we'd get on a bus straight back to the train station. I had to beg initially, though: I'd say, 'I'm going whether you like it or not. I'm going to these courses!' I wanted to get into the acting world and I wanted to dance or sing, so my parents ended up giving in because I was going to do it anyway. I even threatened to run away from home to do it!

There was this café near the studio, on Broadway near the Sydney CBD, that I'd always go to. I loved it; they charged $3.50 for a bowl of spaghetti bolognese. I'd go to Broadway Shopping Centre and buy a gossip magazine, and I loved the time I spent alone like that. I would read the magazine and think I was such an adult, eating my spaghetti bolognese for three-fifty. I also remember giving homeless people any change I had as I walked down to Keane Kids. My parents' generosity has always given me an example of how I should not hang on to every cent I have.

One night I was coming home to Newcastle and the other girls weren't there. I wasn't scared because it was daylight saving. I arrived in Newcastle and from the station I could take one of two buses that would be right out the front. They'd take me to the bus stop at Cardiff Station and my mum would pick me up from there. There was a quick bus, which went direct to Cardiff, and there was a slow bus, which made all the stops, so of course I wanted the quick bus. On these trips everybody would run from the train and I ran out too because I wanted to get on the quick bus each time. I'd stand on the train and think, *As soon as these doors open, I'm bolting.* On this night when I was travelling alone, though, there was an old man standing next to me when the doors opened. He had white-blond hair and was wearing a flannelette shirt. You know those trolleys that older people put all their shopping in, with a little zip at the top? The ones they take wherever they go so they don't have to carry their bags, they can just stroll along? The old man standing next to me had one of those and was trying to get it off the train, without much success. Nobody was helping this poor man off the train and onto the platform, because they were all running to the bus. I could see he was in trouble and I was thinking, *I want to run for this bloody bus, I cannot wait, I'm not going to spend an extra forty-five minutes waiting around for another bus.* But I felt so sorry for him that I picked up his trolley and pulled it over to the platform. I was just starting to take off when he said, 'Thank you, Jakica.' Jakica is my real name, and it's a Croatian name.

However, I didn't register immediately that this man said thank you, let alone that he used my real name. And when I looked back, he was gone. Just – gone. I ran along the platform but missed the first bus, so I ended up on the second bus, sitting there for an extra half an hour, thinking about life and about what I was doing. I realised I was always running and running and running and not having patience for the things that I wanted in life. I think that was the message I was meant to receive from that experience: to slow down, to take my time.

Once I was home I told my mum about this old man, who I'd never seen before in my life, and how he'd known my name. Mum pulled out a photograph of me being held by my paternal grandfather; I was one month old in the photo and only a few months older than that when he passed away. There were two photos of my grandfather in the house and I had never seen them before that day; I'd never seen how my grandfather looked, because my mum had never pulled out photos of my Croatian grandfather. But in that photo he was dressed exactly the same as the old man at the train station.

Needless to say, when Mum showed me this photo she freaked out – in a good way. What had happened was a reassurance that I was being looked after by my grandfather.

* * *

So I loved dancing and singing – and that led to me applying for *Popstars*, the TV show that launched Sophie Monk's career. People have found footage of me auditioning for the show – it's out there somewhere!

When I applied for the show I thought, *This is my chance, this is it, I'm going to get through*. I was speaking to the universe about it the whole time, well before I really knew how that worked. For the audition I wore a pink sparkly hat and pink-tinted sunglasses and I had a pink top with a mohair sort of feel, and a grey skirt and boots. There was someone I knew at the auditions: Tiffany Wood, who went to Johnny Young Talent School with me. She went on to make it into the *Popstars* group, Bardot.

On the audition day for *Popstars* all the cameras were there and all these girls were lined up outside. The cameras stopped at me because I looked like Anastacia with my pink glasses and my mohair top. I said something like, 'You wait till I get in there. I'm coming! My name's Jackie and I will be making it!'

My audition song was Fairground Attraction's 'Perfect'. Jackie O, who is now a well-known radio personality, was one of the judges. As I started singing, Jackie O was looking at me – and I told her many years later, when she interviewed me, that I was on *Popstars*. She said, 'I can't remember that, Jackie,' because she saw so many girls, but I remember her looking at me, and she wanted to put me through.

The judges were all sitting there and looking and thinking, and looking and thinking – and finally they said, 'No.'

My response was, 'Well, this isn't the end of me! You have made a big mistake! You wait, because this face will be seen again. You just wait and see.' It was all on tape – that's how I know exactly what I said. I always had this feeling that I was going to be known. But it wasn't because I wanted to be famous for being famous. I didn't have ambitions for people to be looking at me, or anything like that. I wanted to affect people like Whitney Houston affected me, like the movie *Flashdance* affected me. The way energy moved me in a positive way. There are so many people and things and experiences that have inspired me, and I always knew that I was going to inspire people. That I *wanted* to inspire people. I wanted to connect with people, and, while it may sound corny, I wanted to make their lives better. Life can be tough – for some people it's really tough – and we all need some light. That's what I wanted to do: bring light to people. I just didn't know how. At the time I auditioned for *Popstars* I thought it was going to be through dance or through singing, but now I know differently.

Deep connections

I would have been about four when we lived in the Newcastle suburb of Hamilton. We moved into a flat and next door lived a couple who we came to call Grandma and Grandpa. Grandma basically adopted Mum, although she had two daughters of her own. However, her kids always fought with each other and one of them hadn't talked to her for many, many years. Grandma and Grandpa were part of all our lives for many years – well after the time we moved to Speers Point, which was about five years later. Mum kept the relationship going because they were part of our family, and we were part of theirs, even though we weren't related by blood.

At first one of their daughters liked that Mum was always hanging out with Grandma and that Grandma loved Mum. The other daughter never met Mum but they could both tell that Mum wasn't a threat to them, because she is a really beautiful person. My mother would always go over to Grandma and Grandpa's place; and she always made time for Grandma. She'd talk to her and if she needed any help, Mum would be there. They'd go out to lunch every Thursday, and Grandma would confide in Mum about her relationship with her daughters. When I found out all about this later, it sounded as though it wasn't the most loving situation: the more the daughters were given, the more they seemed to want from Grandma.

Even once we moved to live in Speers Point, Mum still saw Grandma every Thursday; there used to be a mall in Newcastle where you'd go up these escalators and there'd be a little food court, and that was their thing to do together. They'd go out and they'd have lunch, and they used to go and play the pokies too. They'd go to the club and have a little gin and tonic, because my grandmother loved it. She looked forward to those Thursdays with Mum. I'd also visit Grandma regularly until my late teens.

At a certain point, one of the daughters said to Mum, 'Oh, you know Mum's got dementia – it's getting worse.' Mum's response was, 'I don't believe she's got dementia,' because she saw Grandma every week and she knew that Grandma's mind was intact. By this time I was driving – my little Ford Capri – so I'd go over to visit. One day I said, 'Grandma, why are you pretending that there's something wrong with you? I know there's nothing wrong – you don't have dementia.'

She started crying. She said she was tired of her daughters arguing all the time, and she was sick of her husband. By this time Grandma and Grandpa were in their eighties. Grandpa used to be a master builder, so he knew a lot of people. I later found out that he had a lot of pull in Newcastle, and a lot of contacts. He'd had a near-fatal car accident when he was in his forties and I think they had to put a plate in his head; apparently he changed and became more angry. He was never aggressive towards Grandma – he just had a short fuse. Despite Grandma being tired of Grandpa, they decided to hold a party for their fiftieth wedding anniversary. By this time, Mum was quite close to one of their daughters and we were all sitting around at the party when she said to Mum, 'I know you're not going to like this, Lana, but Mum is going straight into a home after this party.' She meant a nursing home. So Grandma and Grandpa had been sleeping together in the same bed for fifty years and now Grandma was going into a home and nobody else knew it was about to happen. Grandma had no idea she was being driven straight to a home after this party – who would do that to their parent? It still makes me angry to think that a child could do that to their mother.

Mum started crying. 'You can't do that,' she said. 'I'll take them in.'

'You're not taking them in, Lana,' Grandma's daughter said.

Mum insisted, 'I *will* take them in, and I don't want money to do it.'

I think that woman and her sister were scared that because Mum was like a daughter to Grandma – and I have cards that showed that I was loved and treated like family by Grandma and Grandpa from the age of five, and my siblings have the same – she was going to ask for money or she was going to take money, even though they knew my mother was not like that.

'You can't do that,' Mum went on. 'You can't just send the man home by himself. He's eighty-three – they've been together for fifty years.' My mother was so upset. And after that party Grandma's daughter did exactly what she said she would. She dropped Grandpa home, saying to him, 'Mum's going into a home and you're going into the house by yourself.' Then Grandpa was crying, saying that they couldn't take Grandma away. But they did and left the man alone in the house.

I was angry, too, because I knew Grandma didn't have dementia – she was just pretending to escape any demands from her family. Not long before that party she'd said to Mum, 'I want to buy the girls something beautiful so they have something to remember me by.' So she bought me these beautiful pearls, which I still have, and she gave pearls to Angela too. Grandma was sharp enough to do that – and to look ahead – but it's as if she knew something was going to happen to her.

When Grandma went into the home it seemed almost as if she didn't care, like she was starting to give up because she couldn't stand her daughters fighting any longer. Even though my mum continued to see her every week and had a strong relationship with her, she had no legal pull – and Mum didn't want to go down that route anyway. But we were the ones who took her out of the home at Christmas, on weekends and for family events. We'd have her stay with us some weekends, and I'd see her at four o'clock in the morning speaking to my baby brother Milan, who was a child then. She would be looking at the stars and speaking to him, and I knew that was her happy place.

Then the daughters started getting upset because I'd go and visit Grandpa; they wanted to put him in a home, too. He said to me, 'Jackie, you're going to help me here.' He had a hernia and there was cancer in his stomach, but he could still look after himself. I took him to the hospital for treatment, though, and he had to be there for a week because it couldn't be managed at home. I visited him the whole time and went to his house to get his clothes.

Even when he was sent home, Mum and Dad and I were the ones bringing him food and cleaning his house. I was there after work every day, making sure he had what he needed, that he was fed. I did his shopping and I'd sit with him while he ate. I even lay in the bed next to him. Sometimes he'd hold my hand and become quite teary.

'It's all right,' I'd say. 'Come on, eat your food.'

While he was in the hospital, his daughters brought in someone to assess him as a precursor to having him put into a home. By then things had become even icier between them and my mother.

I said, 'Mum, we can't let them put Grandpa in a home – we need to do something.' He didn't have dementia; he still had cancer in his stomach but he could get up and walk. The doctors let him continue to live at home. He might not have been able to drive his car but we didn't want him to drive – we could take him wherever he wanted to go. We wanted to look after him, because we loved him just like we loved Grandma.

But they brought in this assessor. 'What the f*** do you want?' Grandpa said – that's how he spoke, even though he was eighty-three. 'You're a rogue like my daughter,' he said. 'F*** off, because I'm not going anywhere. What do you want to know – what day it is?' I was there that day and he demanded to see the piece of paper the assessor was filling in.

'Tell my daughter she's a rogue,' he said, and he wrote that on the piece of paper. 'She's not getting any of my money.'

I said, 'Oh my God, Grandpa, you can't say that!'

But he wrote down that his daughter wouldn't be receiving anything, then told the assessor to piss off. It meant they couldn't put him in a home, though, and every time he was in the hospital the assessor would come back in, but he'd always answer the questions correctly.

After a while, though, Grandpa started to become much more sick, so my dad said, 'Get up, you're coming to live with us.' He was with my parents for about four months, and he loved it. It was a difficult time for all of us, though, because he needed a lot of care, and not all of it was pleasant, because the cancer spread to his bowel and started to cause all sorts of problems. I remember one morning at three o'clock I had to clean him up; he was crying and I wanted to cry as well, but more than that, I wanted to help him. I wanted to wake Mum and Dad so they could help, but instead I said, 'Don't worry, Grandpa.' I felt so horrible for him.

He used to argue with my dad. Dad would yell and Grandpa would say, 'You're a bloody foghorn, Ivan.' Dad would walk off and laugh, or he'd argue back and say, 'Well, at least it keeps your mental state going, doesn't it?' I think the argy-bargy with Dad kept Grandpa pepped up.

Grandpa kept his independence though. He'd still go out on his own when he could. One day he said to me, 'I want you to drop me off somewhere.' I didn't know what he was up to, but I dropped him off in Hamilton. I knew he'd get home all right, because he'd usually take the bus when he wanted to get around, and when he wanted the bus to pull over he'd tap the window with his walking stick. Sometimes he'd have the bus driving right up to the front of our house.

This day, though, he went to a lawyer and he changed everything in his will. I didn't know anything about this at the time and neither did my parents. Nobody forced him to do anything; my grandpa did what he wanted. He always did. Nobody could tell that man what to do, I can tell you that right now.

Then Grandpa went to hospital one last time. Before I left his room – not knowing that I wouldn't see him again – he thanked me.

Later, I was lying on my bed and all of a sudden this bird came flying to my window and it just went *bang*. I heard three taps and I knew it was a spirit. This was before I acknowledged that I was a psychic medium, but I knew what it was.

Then the phone call came and Mum and Dad told me the news. I didn't cry, although it shocked me a bit. After I'd processed the news, the tears came. I knew that bird was Grandpa saying, *Thank you and I'm now free, and I'm happy and I'm at peace.* For me it was the acknowledgement that he had passed on to the next, higher consciousness. So I didn't grieve, because I knew he was happy, and that made me happy. He was home, and he was home with his other family members.

Grandma was still alive at that point, but Mum and I had been prevented from seeing her for quite some time. We tried fighting it but it came to a point that we couldn't fight any more. I didn't get to say goodbye to Grandma.

She did end up getting dementia later on; in some ways this was a blessing because it meant she didn't have to deal with some of the unpleasantness that went on.

I am grateful that I had Grandma and Grandpa in my life, and they gave me and my brothers and sister plenty of love. My parents cared for them, and so did I, and it's the memories of the times we had together that remain.

And that experience underlined so much of what my mother and father taught me my whole life – that it is not money that matters. It is family, friends, caring for each other and kindness. I feel sorry for people who lose sight of that.

Lost and found

There was a time in my life that caused a lot of pain; so much that I don't like to think about it often or reflect on it. It was a time that changed me fundamentally, so I can't say I'd be the person I am today without it – but that still doesn't mean I like to think about it.

Even now I find it hard to write about this. But I have to explain, and share this experience if I am honest about what has shaped me as a person and brought me to this point in my life. For a few years I was involved with a man – let's call him Paul – and during that relationship I lost myself. I travelled a very long way from who I was and it took me quite a while to come back. Maybe that's happened to you too. I know it's happened to a lot of women, and some men. We do things because we love someone and we believe they love us too, and it can take a while to realise that you've been tricked but by then it seems almost impossible to get out.

For the first six months of the relationship with Paul I was still my outgoing self. I was confident, the way I'd been raised to be. Then I started listening to Paul's brainwashing. When I went into the relationship I thought this man loved me, although I realised later that he didn't. But I wanted to make him happy. My parents have had a long marriage and they are loyal to each other; I thought I had to be loyal to this man because we were together.

But Paul would tell me what to wear and how to behave. It happened slowly and so I didn't notice what he was doing. His behaviour gradually became more and more difficult to handle and I started to disappear. He wanted to take everything away from me – and he tried really hard to do it – but there were pockets of me that he couldn't take away. I believe there was something in me saying to myself, *Stand your ground, because if you don't, you're going to marry this man, and there'll be nothing, you'll be sitting in the kitchen crying every day. Not seeing your family. Not having any kind of life.* But even though I look back now and feel like I allowed him to have power over me, I'm proud I held on to enough of myself that eventually I found my way out.

I got into that situation because I was looking for love outside myself. I thought that relationship was love, but I wasn't being authentic, because I knew deep down Paul didn't love me. I knew how terrible he was making me feel. But I was too scared to get out of the relationship because I didn't love who I was and I thought this was a relationship that was valuable. I told myself you just put up with that kind of thing because it was what I had seen – not in my parents' marriage, but in other European marriages where the women would listen to the men.

I believed Paul loved me, and I needed that to help me cope with his behaviour and convince myself that how he behaved was okay because I didn't want him to leave. I was too scared to be by myself. I was a confident chick before I was with him yet I turned into this person who didn't go out on Friday nights because he told me not to. He would threaten me. And I allowed that, because I wasn't being true to who I was.

I lost myself emotionally and spiritually. I didn't want to acknowledge what was going on with the relationship. I wanted to blame everybody else but me. I was blaming God, the universe and my friends, but it was my fault. *I* allowed this to happen, nobody else.

In the end it was my father who forced the issue. After he saw Paul's behaviour up close for the first time, he said to me, 'I didn't raise a daughter to be told what to do by a man. He doesn't love you – get rid of him.'

It's very hard to combat a person who seems to spend so much time and energy controlling you. I had years of fighting it, and it was exhausting. Even now I have triggers from things that used to happen. But I've forgiven him, even if sometimes I don't think I've forgiven myself. I think you really, truly forgive somebody when you don't have any negative emotions left, when you look at a person and you only see them with love and light. And I do see Paul with love and light even though there are still times when I'll think, *I can't believe I allowed that!* It angers me that I did. But if I didn't go through that, I wouldn't be able to sit here and tell you about it, and maybe my story will help you.

If you are in a relationship and feel you have lost who you are, if the person you are with belittles you or emotionally abuses you or physically abuses you, trust that you can find your way out. And take steps to protect yourself while you do. It is hard – but you deserve better. I found forgiveness is not just freeing, you can look people in the eyes and say, 'I have taken my power back and I'm going to continue this journey as a human being.' It took me a long time to get there but it's almost as if the angels knew I would go through all this.

After it was over I would ask myself, 'Did I attract that, or did somehow the energy attract that, for me not to be on my right path?' Because I lost myself. I didn't stand my ground, so I lost my power. I gave it away without acknowledging that I was choosing to give that power away. I lost myself because I wanted to be loved – because I didn't love myself enough. I thought that true love was somebody else loving me, but *true love is loving yourself first.* It took me a long time to realise that. It also took me a long time to acknowledge that I manipulated Paul as well so he would keep loving me. If he said he wanted me to stay home at night, I'd say okay and I did that for a very long time – but then I'd start going out with my girlfriends and I wouldn't tell him. So I was lying to him. Because I wasn't happy. That was a vicious cycle of pretending that this was such a perfect relationship. But by lying to him I was changing who I was. I was turning into somebody I didn't like – a liar. And it was very hard to admit that.

Even after we broke up I begged God to bring me back to this man. After he broke up with me I would go home and cry every night: 'I want to be back with this man. This is the man I want to marry. Why is this happening to me?' I was holding on to the notion that this was what a relationship looked like. He was the only guy who loved me the way I loved him (or so I thought). I loved him so much that I couldn't live without him – or that's what I thought. Yet he wasn't good for me and I knew it, but I didn't love myself enough to release myself from that energy. I didn't know my self-worth. I couldn't make my stand.

At the time, I didn't know what depression was but after that relationship was over I now realise I was in some kind of depressive state. I had thoughts of driving my car off a cliff to make all this pain end. The pain of the break-up was consuming my life.

I was working in a bank at that time – after starting in a corporate bank in Sydney, I had moved into retail banking. It was a means to an end. I'd go to work, I'd come home and I wouldn't come out of my room. I'd be crying all the time, or trying to read books about self-help. But I was begging God every night to bring Paul back, because he was the love of my life (or so I thought). That behaviour went on for a year. All through that time, though, I was speaking to my angels – specifically, to Archangel Michael. You may already know about Archangel Michael; if you don't, trust me when I say that if there's one angel you want to be talking to, it's him.

At the bank where I worked at the time, everybody knew me as the vibrant girl, the confident girl, because

I was always loud. But that was changing: I lost so much weight after the relationship ended and I was really pale. I wasn't eating and I was depressed. My personality had changed. After a month my colleagues wondered what was wrong with me. That was the toll the depression was taking on me, because I might have been out of the relationship but I still hadn't found my self-worth. I wanted Paul back, but I was beating myself up about wanting him back. I know there are a lot of you who will relate to that: you find yourself in a situation that is toxic, and you *know* it's toxic, but you try to perpetuate it because it's what you know, and also because you think it's what you deserve. That relationship had turned me so inside out that I lost myself in it, and it was taking a long time to find my way back.

One night I said to the angels, 'Prove to me – where are you?'

The next day I was at work when a man approached the counter. I said, 'Can I help you?' I didn't say 'Shine it up' like I used to. I didn't look up at him. I wasn't my usual vibrant self.

He handed me a receipt book that had a butt in it which I stamped, but there was no name on it. He said, 'How are you?' I glanced up. He had blond hair and the bluest eyes I'd ever seen, and he had this leather vest on with criss-cross lacing on the front.

He said, 'What do you think you want to do with your life?'

I didn't answer for a second. Then out of my mouth popped: 'I want to work with God.' I thought, *What? I sound like a religious nut.*

He kept looking at me and said, 'Then why don't you?'

It was a Friday afternoon and there was a line out the door, because that's what would happen every Friday afternoon. Then I took the money from him, and when I looked up, he was gone.

That afternoon I went into a newsagency and picked up a pack of tarot cards. This was before I started doing psychic readings, and I had a thought about those: *They're not for you.* Then I went to the back of the newsagency at Marketown and I picked up a pack of cards that had 'Archangels' printed on it. They were already unwrapped so I could look at them. I opened them up – and there was the dude I'd seen at the bank.

Under his image was written: *Archangel Michael.*

I started bawling my eyes out. A few people were looking at me – they were doing their thing, it was Friday afternoon, they were getting their Lotto tickets and what have you. But that was my *a-ha* moment. I've had many of those since.

I bought the cards, got in my car, went home and told my mum. I showed the cards to her and said, 'This is Archangel Michael, the man who I saw.' Mum thought I was cuckoo, but she also knew that I was crying every night and she was worried for me.

When you ask for something and you're given it, and you're given the knowledge that there is something else out there higher than yourself, what are you going to do with that truth? Are you going to have faith? Because I was shown an angel and he talked to me, and I still didn't want to believe what I was seeing. I was still doubting my faith.

After that, however, I started to make some progress, and I was guided to go to a spiritual shop called Angels on the Lake in Newcastle, which is where the whole next phase of my life began – but I'll tell you about that a bit later.

* * *

There have been times when I would say, 'Is there a God? Where are you? I've lost my faith; I need it back and you need to show me.' And when I say 'God', I mean that my

God is universal, not a fixed idea of God from religion. To me, God and the universe are interchangeable.

Whenever I say to God, 'Where are you? Show yourself,' God always does, some way or somehow. Often the person who's asking God to show themselves might not be ready to listen. When I do readings, I find that ninety-five per cent of people are ready to hear but the other five per cent aren't. I've done psychic medium readings where I will tell and tell and tell someone, for example, about a relationship. They'll say, 'I just want him back. He makes me happy.' They don't want to hear what I'm saying. That means they're not ready on a soul level, on an emotional level, on a physical level.

While I was in that relationship where I lost myself, I always had faith in the universe, and part of me was always ready to hear, but the other part of me said, 'I don't want to hear this because it's not what I thought in my head was going to happen.' I was a bit fearful that if I heard what I actually needed to hear, I would detach myself from the victim stance for a second and then I would be forced to acknowledge that I was responsible for everything that was going on and that I needed to make that move. *That* is so often the hardest thing to acknowledge: that you have responsibility for your own life and you have to *take responsibility* for your own life. If you're going to claim the good things you also have to claim the bad. You have to be willing to listen to what the universe is saying to you when you've asked it for help.

I believe spirit comes in many different forms, so that you feel comfortable with what you're seeing. One time an angel appeared to me and it was a bumblebee. I almost felt like I was in a different consciousness when I saw it – but a consciousness where I felt safe. And the message I heard in my mind was, *You have a bigger purpose – you must help people.* That was a message I knew was always there. The voice I heard was my voice; it wasn't a separate voice. It was like there was no separation, no time and space separating me from the universe, so of course it was my voice – because my voice was connected to every living thing.

When that happened, I remember jumping off my bed feeling electrified and inspired. I was in awe of what was happening, but at the same time it was like I was home. I truly believe that God presented this angel to me in a way that wouldn't make me feel fearful, in the same way that God presented the ponies to me when I was a child. Seeing the stars around those little ponies with the coloured tails, purples and pinks and golds, was comforting. Archangel Michael came to me in the bank because he knew that I wouldn't freak out seeing a man with the bluest eyes you've ever seen and the blondest, straightest hair.

I have been told by spirit that when we pass on to the next consciousness level we have a life review of everything we've ever thought, positively, negatively; of the way we've treated people – and every human being has treated a person negatively somewhere in their life, even if it was someone who pissed you off on the bus. In this life review of everyone who you've ever made feel good about themselves or negative about themselves, you feel what you did to them – you actually feel their joy or their pain.

As my life has gone on there have been many times when I've said, 'Is there a God?' and I've prayed. And I do pray. I pray in my bedroom. And there have been times when I have walked into a church and lit a candle. It makes me feel very calm. I'm not being forced to go into a church; it depends on how I feel in that moment.

I get a lot of peace from my angels and the saints. I believe that a lot of the saints who lived carry on into the next consciousness to help people like you and me get on our right path. And every time we get off it, there are little forks in the road, and we take different directions depending on how we're feeling emotionally.

It really comes down to knowing that you are never, ever alone and all you have to do is reach out and ask, and know that your prayers are being heard and answered at the *right* time, rather than on *your* time. Things were about to change for me in a very positive way. It was the right time.

Being a psychic medium

I feel I have been given not the gift of psychic ability, because I believe everyone has that gift, but the gift of being able to tell people things, to help them find their right path. I'm just a normal chick from Newcastle; I'm like anybody else, I've had the same sorts of experiences as everyone else. I come from a very humble beginning, I didn't grow up with a lot of money, and I've worked hard.

I used to tell myself that there was something more in this world that I needed to do and I knew I was going to be known for it. I always knew that it was going to be something big even though I didn't know what that 'big' was. All I knew was that I had to move forward with it.

In the aftermath of the end of my relationship with Paul, my mental health wasn't good but my life was pretty straightforward: go to work, do my time in the bank, come home. There was no sense that there was something else there for me – no extra dimension to my experience – until the day Archangel Michael walked into the bank and I was guided to Angels on the Lake in Newcastle, a three-minute drive from my parents' house. It stocked books about self-help; it had stones, crystals and all those sorts of spiritual things. You've probably been into a shop like it.

The first time I walked into the shop the owner was there and I started to get psychic vibes from her – I was just picking up on things about her and telling her what they were. She was probably surprised that I was so forthcoming, but I just felt I had to tell her. I was wondering, *How is it that I know these things?* And she was in shock that I knew her family members who had passed away and things that she was going through emotionally, physically and spiritually.

She mustn't have been put off by what she heard, though, because she asked me to work in the shop. My exact reply was, 'I'm not working in your shop as a psychic. I'm not a psychic, mate. I work in banking.'

I left her standing at the counter and went to look at the books, because I was still working through a lot of stuff after the end of my relationship and wanted advice, and a book fell right in front of me as if someone had pushed it out. It was called *Divine Guidance* by Doreen Virtue. I opened it and the passage on the first page I saw showed me how to differentiate between true guidance and false guidance. I popped it back on the bookshelf and went home.

The next day I returned to the bookshop and the owner asked me again, 'Will you work here as a psychic?' And I said no, again. But I bought that book and went home.

I went back again the next day. The owner asked, 'Will you work as a psychic?'

'Yes,' popped out of my mouth, as if someone else was accepting the job for me. It wasn't me saying it; it was spirit – it had to be, because I thought, *What am I doing saying yes?*

The next day she had two people for me to give a psychic reading to, although I'd never given one before in my life. But I knew I was speaking to spirit, I was speaking to angels, well before that first moment in the shop happened. I had done it since childhood.

After my first reading I was booked out for a month. Then I was booked out for two months, four months

– six months. All on word of mouth. If the women who worked there asked how I was feeling each day I'd say, 'We're shining it up anyway, so it doesn't matter.' Or, 'It's okay, I'm shining it up anyway.' That was my mantra to get me through what were still difficult days, because although I was starting to turn a corner, I was still having problems with the fact my relationship was over.

Doing those readings was the thing that started to pull me out of my depression, little bit by little bit, because they brought my faith back. I started not thinking about Paul so much. I started reading my books and learning more about why I was in this situation. I read and read and read. I was reading Wayne Dyer and Doreen Virtue, all of these books about manifestation and Archangel Michael and the power of the subconscious mind. I'd be sitting in my room and Dad would be knocking on the door for me to come out – he was worried about me. I didn't want to be around anyone. For two years I didn't tell my dad that I was giving readings because I was scared of what he would say about this new path I was taking. But lots of people started to know about me – people were coming from Sydney and interstate to get readings. I thought Dad wouldn't find out – even though the shop was so close to home.

So I was gradually emerging from the state I was in. God was telling me: *You think there's no answer but the universe is responding to your every thought, and now it's up to you what you're going to do with this.*

So I went to a different shop and gave the woman there a reading; the shop sold knick-knacky things and the woman's husband was well known around Newcastle. As I started her reading I said her father had passed away and mentioned how it had happened; I named her grandmother – all sorts of things that come up during a reading. She freaked out and said, 'How do you know all these things?' And I said, 'I'm psychic. I just know.'

After I'd been doing readings for a while, I even said to Archangel Michael, 'My mother thinks I'm going cuckoo, she thinks I'm having some kind of breakdown.' Then I said to God, 'You want me to be a psychic? If I'm going on this path after all that crap with that man, I need my mum to believe in what I'm doing and you need to prove it to her.' Because I needed my mum's support – if she believed in me I knew I had the power and the strength to do the work. And the first thing I heard was what I needed to do: *Go and tell your mum about the psychic reading you just gave this woman.* So I told her and, without me knowing, the next day Mum walked into that shop.

'Did a young lady come in yesterday?' she asked the owner, and the woman said, 'Is that your daughter? She is so gifted. She could not know the things she knew. There's no way – you can't google it. You should be so happy that you have this psychic for a daughter.'

Mum was thinking, *Is this really true? Jackie's not having a breakdown? Maybe she's coming out of her depressive state.*

Mum was still doubting the work I was doing, and my abilities, but I said to God, 'If my mum doesn't believe it, I'm not doing it. The one person I need to have supporting me is my mother. If she supports me, I can do it. I can put myself in front of anybody and everybody.'

One day I was lying on the lounge while Mum was cooking in the kitchen nearby. 'I'm going to give you a little vibe – a little reading,' I said.

She said, 'All right.'

I said, 'In the next half an hour you'll go to the toilet and you're going to pee and you're going to have blood in your urine, and you're going to discover you have an infection and that is proof that I'm psychic. Archangel Michael is telling me to tell you right now.'

She looked at me as if to say, *This is ridiculous*, and it probably did sound that way to her.

But my mother went to the toilet and what I said would happen, happened. Of course, she freaked out. She went to the doctor the next day, and they said she had what I'd said she had. From that moment she was in. She knew that this was real, that I was being truthful.

That was the pinnacle for me because I had the support of my mother, and it was very important to me to have her support. Because my mother's very much like me: if she dreams something, it happens.

My mother's belief in me started bringing my faith back. So did learning that I had created this out of all my challenging experiences – that's what the universe showed me. It was about acknowledging that we as human beings go through these experiences, good and bad, and I needed to take responsibility for the situation that I had created or allowed.

The universe knew – and so did I, deep down – that if I married Paul I would have lost myself and I wouldn't be doing this work now – I'd be sitting in a kitchen cooking and cleaning and crying over a man who treated me badly. And that's just not me. I believe the universe responded to those subconscious thoughts. The spirits knew that I'd be crying over a man who was going to take me away from my purpose. But that was the bigger picture – it was what needed to happen.

* * *

Giving someone a reading takes a lot of energy and focus, and it can also leave the psychic medium giving the reading quite vulnerable. When I started doing readings, I knew Archangel Michael would protect me. And I also protect myself by envisaging a white light around me. So I've never had experiences where a negative energy has attached itself to me during or after a reading.

However, there have been about four occasions when the energy knew that I was about to help people or stay on my path – almost like a dream state – and they've tried to come in and prevent me from doing that. On those occasions I hadn't protected myself before I went to sleep at night – and it's during dreams that something might happen.

I always had a feeling that I would be able to affect people in a positive way. Music affects people, art affects people, people affect people, people inspire people, and obviously no one needs to be in the public eye to affect people and inspire people because I was already doing that before I appeared on television. Before I joined *The Real Housewives of Melbourne* I had an extensive waiting list as a professional psychic medium. So I was already known in New South Wales as this psychic medium in demand but that was not because of publicity. I didn't put myself in the papers, I didn't do interviews; it was all through word of mouth. The universe made this happen so quickly that it's as if when Archangel Michael came into the bank that day and I said I wanted to work with God, I wasn't aware of how soon I'd discover the gifts that were waiting for me.

I have to say – and I really believe this – that I don't have more special psychic medium abilities than anyone else. I'm just more trusting of what I hear; I trust every single thing that comes to my mind and I believe that's the reason my accuracy is so high when I give psychic medium readings. I trust everything I hear through spirit.

Many people have said to me over the years, 'When I hang out with you my energy is heightened,' which I know sounds weird – except it really isn't. Some friends, and people who have spent some time with me, have said, 'I don't know how it is, but my psychic ability is heightened. I am able to hear things much more, I'm able to feel the energy, I'm more aware. I don't know why but I can feel the way you feel things, Jackie.' They tell me that when they take the advice of what spirit guides or angels have told them through me, it not only makes them feel better about the issues they're experiencing but also something shifts, and they feel more at peace.

So, how do my psychic abilities work? When I meet somebody or see somebody, I see their past, their present and their future – automatically. I start to see information about their life and what they've gone through. It's like a movie flash in my mind. I read their thoughts and I feel their feelings. When I give a psychic reading, or if I'm out and about and I haven't turned my energy off, I will literally start feeling the aches and pains of the people around me. When I give a psychic medium reading I always tell my clients that I will usually connect with whoever has passed away and needs to come through, but it's like I'm actually sitting in your physical body and I'm feeling all your aches and pains. I'm a vessel for the messages that are coming through.

When my life was starting to come on track in a positive way – when my spiritual path had really started – I was lying in my bed one night and I opened my eyes and rolled over, and I saw this girl standing next to my bed; she had short black hair. She didn't scare me. I was coming out of my dream state, I was half awake. I thought, *What are you doing?* I put my hand through her but she just smiled at me. I said out loud, 'Oh, what are you doing?' Then I realised with a shock that it was a spirit standing there. And I said to my angels, 'You want me to do this work? Do not put spirits like that in front of my face ever again! It freaks me out!' So I'm very good at seeing spirits when my eyes are closed. Or if I look at you and I see the image of the spirit with my third eye. I don't want to see spirits walking past you when I have my eyes open. It would be a lot harder for me to work that way! Nor do I want to be walking down the street and see spirits walking by. My angels are very conscious of not letting me see that, so that's why I talk about seeing images with my third eye.

There was one memorable reading that I gave early in my psychic medium days. It was at Angels on the Lake and the readings were done in the back of a cupboard – well, the room was so small that it felt like a cupboard; it was where they stored excess stock and that kind of thing. So I was in this small space, sitting on a chair, and all of a sudden everything went black. My eyes were open but all I saw was black.

I thought, *My god, what is going on here?* Because I was blind – I couldn't see anything. I started freaking out, understandably. Then I said, internally, *Angels, help me*. I closed my eyes as I was saying it.

Just as quickly as it started, I came out of it, almost as if time had frozen for a second. The woman I was giving the reading to looked at me and said, 'Are you okay?' I said, 'Yes, but I just went through something that I believe you've gone through. Did you experience a situation where you went completely blind or you couldn't see for a short period of time?'

She said, 'Yes, I was in a coma.' She had been in an accident when she was driving a car and blacked out at the wheel. Not many people knew about that, except for close family and friends.

I freaked out during that reading because in every single reading I do I usually have control – I do not lose control of my energy. But in that moment I was not in control of what was going on, I realised how strong my connection with people was – and also that I was being protected, because my experience was temporary. But the angels were allowing me to feel what that person was feeling, to feel their energy, so I could help them.

After I'd been doing readings at Angels on the Lake for a while, I decided to work for myself. This was a massive thing to do at the age of twenty-six, because I didn't know how it would turn out. But I was working on manifesting abundance – that was a personal practice, just for me – and I knew that I needed to move on and not work for someone else. At the same time my angels were in my head saying, *It's time for you to leave this little safety net and shine on, create your next step.*

Well before I made that decision I had visualised the place where I wanted to live: a house on the waterfront, big enough for me to live in and work from. I was very specific: I wanted to be able to go on the roof deck of this house and see all of Lake Macquarie. If you've ever been to Newcastle you would have driven past this particular place because it's right on the esplanade coming from Toronto into Speers Point. A big part of manifesting that home was believing that I deserved to have it – and that belief is something we all struggle with at times, but I knew what I wanted to bring into my life. My mother and a family friend were going to help me set up my new working arrangements, so I just needed the house – and when I found it, I rented it.

I started doing my readings there. I've always said that whoever is meant to come in for a reading will come in and my angels will tell me if somebody is a non-believer before I give them a reading. As far as I'm concerned, everyone is the same when they come to me for a reading; people from all walks of life have come to see me and it doesn't matter what their background is, or what their lifestyle is like, they're all equal. Although I do sometimes think people from particular walks of life are brought into my orbit so that I can learn how to deal with different situations and individuals. Certainly, some of the people who come to me for readings have things in their lives that I have never experienced and likely never will – but I'm interested in everyone, and every single person has a story.

There was a lady who would come in maybe once a year; I wouldn't allow people to come back every two months or anything like that. If I give you a reading, you have to take responsibility for what I've told you, you have to put that into practice and listen to your own intuition to create your life. I am here purely to help you along with that, I'm not somebody you keep coming back to every two months or three months because you can't handle your life and you need answers. That is not how I roll.

So this woman would come back every year for a refresh of her reading. I don't usually remember what I say during readings – I'm delivering the information, and it leaves me as soon as I've conveyed it. But I know what happened during one of her readings because this woman told me the story later.

She had a son and she was divorced from her son's father. She wanted her son to come to me for a reading when he was seventeen years old; I told her that nobody is allowed to have a reading before they're eighteen – that's my rule. When the boy walked in once he'd turned eighteen, I didn't know he was her son. I started the reading and said, 'Oh, your dad's here,' and I started acknowledging how his father was killed – the son would have known the details, of course, but I didn't know.

As it happened, I had seen this when his mother had been in for a reading of her own, but I didn't remember it. I told her that her ex-husband was coming through; I named him, I named how he died, I named the woman who died with him and what had happened to them. My client had wanted her son to come for a reading because she knew that I could help him, that he would be able to talk to his dad and acknowledge what had happened. I'd be able to tell him things that nobody knew and give her son the peace he needed. Because she'd been coming to me for readings for a while she knew that she could trust everything I saw.

I could see that the deaths of her ex-husband and the woman who was with him were made to look as if one had killed the other then themselves, but that's not what actually happened.

'That's not the case,' I said to the son. 'They're here and they're apologising for what's happened.' I named his father and told the boy things his father wanted him to know. One thing in particular I remember: 'There is twenty-five thousand dollars rolled up in notes in a back shed that's white,' I said, 'connected to the house where he was murdered. People are looking for it. It's behind an axe in a blue plastic bag behind a false brick.'

I couldn't believe I was saying this stuff – I was just blurting it out because it was coming from the father, coming from his spirit. And I wasn't aware of it at the time; I was told all the details later.

'You need to tell your godfather,' I said, not knowing – but finding out later – that the godfather was involved in a few things that might have made him a person you don't want to upset.

The boy said, 'Oh, okay,' probably because what I was saying wasn't too shocking to him – and he probably liked the idea of finding that much money!

I then forgot all about it, because that's what happens after a reading; I certainly didn't remember what I said to him.

Sometime later I was living by the beach, something else I had visualised and manifested: moving from the lake to the beach. I was still working from home, and on this day I was sitting in my room meditating. I remember hearing these motorbikes roll up, and then a man wearing leathers walks in. My mother was working with me, so she was there. And she's not naïve at all, but I don't think she'd ever seen a man like this before.

When he walked in my heart stopped for a second, because he looked as if he was going to shoot me.

'Who's Jackie?' he said to Mum.

'I'm Jackie,' I said. 'Are you here for a reading?'

He stared at me.

'You're here for a reading, are you?' I said again.

He looked at me as though he was going to try to intimidate me – but I could see through it.

'Come in,' I said. And what I meant was, *When you come into my room, mate, nobody puts it over me. I will smash you with the truth in a way that's going to affect you.*

He sat down and said, 'Are you a dog?' Meaning, was I a police informant.

I said 'What?' He was getting agitated, so I added, 'You'd better calm yourself because otherwise I won't give you a reading – and I won't be threatened like that.'

He was still staring at me, and he said, 'How did you know my best friend was murdered unless you work with the Feds or the cops? How do you know that there's twenty-five thousand dollars rolled up in a blue bag?' He wasn't yelling at me but it was close.

I said, 'I don't know what you're talking about, mate.'

'The money that you told my godson was in a shed in a blue plastic bag, he rang me up and told me and I didn't believe him,' the man says. 'So I went into that shed and found that money.'

'You've got to stop now,' I said, 'because I have to give you a reading. I've got people coming through.'

Although I don't remember exactly what I said to this man, I do remember that he started to cry.

'I'm not afraid of anyone,' he said. 'I've been shot at. I've had a gun to my head. But the thing that rattles me more than anything is knowing there is no way in this world you could have known any of this.' He stopped speaking and looked at me. 'I need to get out of this life I'm in,' he said, 'because now I know there's a God.'

Whatever I said to him, that moment triggered something in him and he was so affected by it, so rattled by it, that he decided to make a huge change. He was around sixty but he wanted to make that change. I need to be clear, too: *I* didn't do anything that would make him change – I just told him what I heard. But that's the power of the work I do, and it's happened more than once, that someone will decide to change their life radically after having a reading.

* * *

On another occasion I received a phone call from a police officer I had given a reading to when I was still at Angels on the Lake. The woman who owned the shop said, 'You've got five minutes before the next reading, and you need to take this phone call because this woman has lost her husband.'

I took the call and the caller told me the missing man's name and said, 'Where is he?' It wasn't the usual sort of reading I give – I don't want to work with the police because I do not want to work with the dark energies around crimes like murder. There are some psychics who do it, but it's not for me – even though at one stage, when I was younger, I wanted to be a criminologist.

As soon as this caller told me her husband's name I saw the man ready to jump off the cliff at Mount Sugarloaf. 'He's placed his ring down,' I said. 'And he's left a note because he's going to commit suicide.' It was so clear.

'I have to get off the phone,' I said. 'You're going to find him but it's not going to be you who finds him, it's going to be his brother.'

When I hung up the phone, I prayed: 'God, do not let this person take his life. He's got kids and he's got a wife. Don't let him do it!'

Then I closed my eyes and felt energy pull this man back. I remember it so clearly – it wasn't me pulling him back, although I was connecting to him.

I didn't hear anything for about a month, then a man who had booked a reading with me walked into the shop. As he was sitting there I felt his energy and I started rattling off whatever the spirits wanted to tell him.

At the end he said, 'I was about to jump off the cliff at Mount Sugarloaf and nobody knew where I was. You described where I was and you said my brother would find me. My brother knew where we used to go when we were younger, and he took off straight up to Mount Sugarloaf.'

This man worked with emergency services. His job had become too much for him, seeing how many people die, some of them young people who have died because they were doing something reckless. It all became too much for him. He'd been suffering from depression but nobody knew that; on top of his existing mental health issues, it all became too much.

He told me that when he was about to jump from Mount Sugarloaf he felt someone grab him by the back and pull him away, calling his name.

I teared up after he left. *This is what I'm here to do*, I thought. *We're here to help one another, not disconnect from one another. This is why I'm doing what I'm doing.*

* * *

There have been a few times in my life where somebody has tested my psychic abilities during a reading. When I worked out what was going on, I challenged them about it and said, 'You need to get up and leave – I'm not giving you a reading.'

Of course, they'd generally refuse to leave.

'What I give is a gift,' I said to these people. 'It doesn't matter if I charge money – I know what I'm giving you is going to help you. And I know my self-worth. If you don't want to pay for it, nobody is forcing you – you can shine away.'

That comes from knowing that I'm going to be protected when somebody is coming in to test me because of their own ego or their own projections. I'm sure these people wanted to prove that I was a fraud – or thought they could try. Or maybe they were scared that there might really be something else out there, some extra dimension to our existence that they didn't want to acknowledge.

They may also not have liked that I was still young and doing well at my business. If they'd stopped being envious of other people and stopped putting people down, they might have had the time and energy to work out what they were passionate about, so they could follow their own path and follow their own purpose in life. It's so tempting to focus on what other people have and what they are doing – it can seem easier to do that than to make yourself shine. To *let* yourself shine. But it's a waste of your energy and it doesn't achieve anything, ever. How many people do you know who spend their lives being mean towards or about other people while also being successful, whether that's success in work or relationships? I doubt you know any. If you're toxic towards other people you're toxic towards yourself – that energy goes both ways.

Unfortunately, one person who tried to test me in a reading would not let it go. Around the time I became engaged to my husband, Ben, two young women came in for a reading. They told me the reading was amazing – there were lots of compliments. Not long afterwards I was sent a letter saying that I was a fake, although it wasn't put as politely as that. When I read it, I started to get a real feeling of anxiety. My first instinct was that something was not right – that the person who wrote the letter was somebody who knew somebody else who was trying to get at me out of jealousy.

I found out that one of those young women was my
fiancé's ex-girlfriend. That relationship had been over
for a while by the point he and I even started seeing
each other. I couldn't understand why they, or she,
would have a problem with me but it seemed as though
they did.

I answered the letter, and said that I stood by what
I had told them in the reading. I always stand by
everything I say. That doesn't mean there aren't things
I pick up in one reading that sound similar to someone
else's reading. Every human being has similarities with
their bodies and with their emotions. If, for example, I
happen to pick up that you've got an ache on the right-
hand side of your neck and I give a reading to your mum
or to a friend or even to somebody else you don't know,
I may well pick up energy in that area as well. That's
because we all have trigger spots where negativity sits
in the body. There are only so many places for the body
to store emotions – to store emotional pain – whatever
form it takes. That's because our bodies all have the
same muscles, bones and organs, and we all experience
a very similar range of emotions. So two friends who
come to see me in separate readings might think I'm
saying the same thing to each of them, but I'm actually
not: they just happen to have the same problems going

on. In this case, though, I knew it was a set-up and the women just wanted to belittle me.

And there are cases when I have done readings for people who I can clearly and completely see are manipulators – they lie to my face. To them I say, 'You've got to stop lying. I can see it in your psyche – I'm giving you a reading and you're lying to me.'

There are times when I say that and I can tell the person is thinking, *How the hell do you know that?* I will say to them, 'I know you're thinking, *How does she know that?*' and they'll say, 'Yes, I am.'

'I know because I'm in your headspace,' I'll say, because that's how deep energy goes when I give a reading. And, I have to say, I do still freak myself out that I know things like people's names, situations and events in their past. That's because I listen to my gift and I believe it's my responsibility to share it.

* * *

When I was young I used to always see numbers everywhere and I would think, *What is this?* I used to think it meant something but I didn't know what. It wasn't until my spiritual path started to become very prominent and I used to see 111 or 444 or 333 over and over again that I was guided to another book by Doreen Virtue called *Angel Numbers*. I still see angel numbers, but now I know how to interpret them.

I could be watching a television show and I might see the number 63 and a star next to it, and it would mean I'd be praying for a certain thing. The problem I have with praying for things, though, is that while I have all this faith, I want things to happen yesterday! The biggest challenge for me is patience, because I have none. I want everything yesterday even though I know it all happens on the universe's time.

I used to see 111 around the place constantly, and in Doreen Virtue's book I discovered that 111 means that you need to keep focusing your thoughts positively – that is, look at what you're thinking when you are asking for something. If you have a negative thought flip it to positive and keep it positive. For a lot of us, every day, our thoughts are more negative than positive – that might be true for you too. It can be hard to avoid, because we seem to be conditioned to think about the bad more than the good, and it's never a helpful habit – but it's especially not helpful if you're trying to manifest something. You might be putting that intention to the universe and in the meantime you're thinking negatively. You can't then be surprised if you don't have a positive outcome.

I started to see signs that numbers were a reflection of the angels speaking to me. Because I'm not always meditating and the messages aren't always clear, there would be physical signs. They could be numbers or they could even be somebody speaking to me, turning around to say, 'Jackie, what a shiny day today,' and I'd know it was a reminder to keep those thoughts positive.

When you see something repeatedly, it's the spirit talking to you. There was one time I remember, not long after I broke up with Paul, when I was driving my car and I was angry while I was doing it, although I can't remember exactly what I was angry about. It was a Saturday night and I was going out for the night. I was driving down this street that goes into Hamilton and there was a billboard that I always saw on the corner – there would be messages on it that would change regularly. One day there might be an ad for a real estate agency and then it might be an ad for a petrol station.

As I was driving, I was saying, 'Where the hell are you, angels?' I'm always direct with them! But I was upset, too – crying and yelling at them.

Suddenly someone blew in my ear, although my windows were shut, so I knew it wasn't a breeze. But somebody was blowing hard in my ear and I heard the word 'Look' in my head.

I looked to the right and the billboard read: *Keep the faith – it's happening.*

It wasn't numbers that time, but it was a reminder that I was being looked after.

It's up to you to pay attention and understand the universe's messages.

* * *

The work I do is uplifting, and I love it. But there is a down side sometimes: I can be vulnerable to what I can only describe as psychic attacks. We all have a shadow self – a dark side – but there are also dark energies or entities that can try to attach themselves to us. Even though I take steps to protect myself, and I know that the angels protect me, working as a psychic medium does make me vulnerable to negative energy from time to time.

The negative energy is a physical experience for me. There are times when I've been scared, but I will talk to Archangel Michael and I will say to the negative energy, 'Go away,' and I will pray to Archangel Michael. Usually, within a few moments it has gone.

Negative energy is something that anyone who taps into their psychic abilities needs to be aware of, so they can protect themselves. When you connect with people and energy the way I do – the way we all can if we connect with our angels – you're opening a channel to that other person, so you can offer empathy and understanding. Not everyone you connect with will be kind, though, or respectful.

I know I'm not the only person who's had experiences like that – you might have too. There may be a house where you know you're not welcome, where there's an energy that tries to move you out. It could be a person you meet who drains you, so that you always feel tired around them. If you're sensitive to energy, you're sensitive to good *and* bad energy. The first step towards protecting yourself is to be aware of it.

Those experiences are not, of course, enough to put me off the work I do. Even if they're unpleasant, they're rare. I know I'm doing the work I was meant to do, and I know that by doing it I help people. That is a great privilege.

Manifesting an abundant life

Well before I first entered Angels on the Lake and began my work as a psychic medium, I was manifesting my thoughts into reality. I created my first vision board in my late teens. I thought it was normal and that everybody did it. Of course, now I know they don't – but I think they should. You should. *Everyone* should have a vision board. And it's fun! A vision board is a way of representing all the things you want to manifest in your life and it is a very powerful tool.

After I got into and out of that toxic relationship and ended up in a depressive state, I screamed at the universe, 'If there is a God, prove it now, because I'm going through all this crap, I'm listening to everything everybody's telling me to do.' As you know by now, I'm not above screaming at God and the angels. That's when I heard a clear message: *You have a bigger purpose and you must help other people.* The voice didn't come from me, but I felt incredibly connected to the source of it. I can't even truly describe the feeling except to say it was like my mother hugging me a million times over. My consciousness was connected to the universal consciousness. It was an energy of knowing I was one with the universe in that moment, and I was being given a message.

Not long afterwards, a thought popped into my head: *Put the pictures of all the things you want in your life on a board and you will have them.* My mother used to tell me, 'You're not going to have these things – you have to get your head out of the clouds,' and I'd say, 'Watch me. Everything on my vision board I will have.' And to this day, I have everything. From love and saying I wanted a relationship, to friends and family to lifestyle to houses, to inspiring people, being on TV to reach a larger audience, my Shine It Up tours – even the holidays I've taken. Nobody believed in it but I did.

I thought it into existence. That's what manifesting is. I believe that your brain is a magnet for all that you see, whether it's negative, positive, half-negative or half-positive. All that you think is all that you will create, and they're the experiences you will have.

When I give anybody a reading I say, 'I don't know what's going to come out. I don't remember what comes out during a reading because I'm just the vessel to relay the messages. Your angels tell me exactly what to tell you and they're going to be straighty-one-eighty.' There are a lot of people who don't want to take responsibility for where their life is – that is, the parts they can control. Many of our life experiences are the result of where we've put ourselves. And so I tell people that. Or the angels tell them that, because I am just the conduit.

If somebody comes to me for advice even when I'm not doing a reading and says, 'I want this kind of lifestyle,' I say, 'First of all, do you want the lifestyle out of ego or out of the right intentions towards other people? Because if it's out of ego you're not going to get it. Second thing, if you want a loving relationship you have to love yourself in order to attract it. Whether you want to be with a woman or a man, the only way you can manifest the life that you seek is by giving gratitude, doing things with the right intent, and knowing how what you're manifesting is going to help others.'

When I said I wanted to manifest a house, it wasn't just about having a house for the sake of it or to prove that I could: I knew that by manifesting a house I was going to help my family, I was going to help charity, I was going to help my parents, I was going to help the person I'm with. It was a collective consciousness of helping others, not getting the house so I can say, 'Look at me, I have this amazing house.' It was knowing that I was going to share that abundance with other people. The problem with people attaining the life they want is that they're selfish about why they want it. That's the wrong intent, and that's why they don't usually end up with what they want. Even if they do get what they want in the short term, they are unable to hold onto it. Changing that starts by realising that you're not the centre of the universe, so the things you want won't ever be just about you – they will always involve other people. The choices we make in our life have an impact on the people we love.

What's good for you should be for the good of all, but knowing what's good for you means that you have to be truthful. Years ago, I saw J-Lo with a pink diamond ring and for me it vibrated love. I told myself I was going to have a pink diamond ring, not because I wanted a diamond. It was because when I looked at that pink diamond it radiated the love that I wanted to radiate to my partner and other people, because pink represents love to me. That ring may not have been a sign of lasting love for J-Lo but it is definitely the symbol of lasting love for me. And my husband proposed to me with a pink diamond ring.

When people say what their heart's desire is, they're often not being truthful to themselves. They might be in a romantic relationship that's dishonest. In a work situation that's dishonest. Or trying to control a person they're with. You can't collectively manifest a situation in which you control your partner or the people at your work. Negativity will not bring you what you want. You can't say, 'I want to be the manager, and once I am I'm going to do some damage, because of the way people have treated me in the past' – although some people do say that and think that, because they want to take some sort of revenge for what's going on in their lives. But the universe can see beyond the bullshit – and that's all it is – of wanting this. You're not doing it to help others, you're doing it only to help yourself, you're doing this out of ego, not with the right intent. So that's why a lot of people don't have the life they truly want to have, and they may not like hearing that but it's the truth. They haven't taken responsibility for the kind of energy they're sending out in order for good things to come back to them. I learnt that personally and now try to spread that message professionally.

Intent is everything when you're trying to manifest what you want. People who don't get what they want, or in the way they think they want it, need to ask themselves are they doing it out of selfishness and ego, and not from the true intent of their heart? And are they taking responsibility for what's not working for them? For example, I stayed in a toxic relationship because I thought that was what love was about – that the fact I was in a relationship was more important than it being a good relationship. I allowed myself to be beaten down and stayed in the situation rather than acknowledging to myself that it wasn't truthful. I know women who say, 'I'm going to live with a man who's cheating on me because my diamonds look amazing on my fingers and the house that I'm living in looks amazing to my friends, so that makes me happy. But I'm really not happy because I'm drinking or I'm doing drugs or I'm crying every night over my husband who doesn't love me, but I don't want to leave him because it's not going to look good to the community. And I'm going to use my kids as an excuse as to why I'm not going to leave because I don't want to break up a family and I don't have the money to leave.' Dishonesty like this doesn't just impact on that one person – it infects everything. The kids are already seeing what you're doing even if you think you're hiding it. By staying in that situation you're not teaching them how to live a truthful, honest and fulfilling life.

So many people ask me, 'How is it that you're able to change your thoughts about a situation that's quite negative in your life and turn it around?' We all have ups and downs but there was a time in my life when I didn't want to get out of bed and I didn't want to see anybody – that's what I was able to turn around. I always talk about taking responsibility – it is *fundamental* to take responsibility for your actions, because if you don't, you can't change your reality. You'll also always be vulnerable to the control of other people who will try to take that responsibility for you. In other words: if you don't control your life, someone else will. I change my thoughts by taking responsibility for my actions and deciding that I am going to make that change.

There's another element, too: changing your lifestyle. That means removing yourself from toxic people, removing yourself from toxic situations, removing yourself from things that drain you and things that don't add to you and things that don't actually inspire you. Excessive drinking or drug-taking rob people of their energy and focus. You need to be honest with yourself to confront what is holding you down. That could be bad habits or bad people. And I know from personal experience that it is harder to do that than not. When you've hung out with people for a long time or done the same thing over and over for a long time, and you finally decide, 'Yes, I need to make this change,' sometimes it feels like an ending, and not in a good way. It's cutting off a part of your life that doesn't serve you any more but that doesn't mean it isn't traumatic, because it's almost like you have Stockholm syndrome: you've been doing this for so long you're convinced it's the right thing. You'll resist changing what you're used to, and that's a natural human response; you'll even resist changing what you know is bad for you, and that's normal too. But if you want to live the life you *truly* want, you have to do it.

I'm not asking you to do anything that I haven't done myself. I'm hoping that my experiences and what I've learnt from them will help you not have to go through the same things I did. And I can tell you that when you go through this kind of change and get rid of the toxic elements in your life, you'll see a positive effect and wonder why you didn't listen to yourself sooner. But don't be too hard on yourself about that: fear of change and fear of the unknown stop us making those transformations, even when they're necessary. But when you know that the adjustment is going to be positive – and you will know, because we all do know, deep down, who and what is toxic in our lives – you actually have to make that adjustment and be consistent with it. In my case, taking myself out of toxic situations, toxic environments and staying away from things that didn't add to a positive sense of myself really helped me to align much more clearly with my higher self.

Doing readings for so many years, I have learnt that people don't like change. People like an environment where they feel safe. Some women and men have had the same partner since high school, then they get married – not because they're happy in the relationship but because they prefer to stay in it rather than get out of it and be alone. Or they think, *This is going to be disastrous because nobody else is going to love me.* That was me. Or maybe it's going to be too much of a change to their lifestyle: they won't be able to live in the same house or the same suburb or whatever it is. There are always reasons to resist change, but if you're not happy in the circumstances you're in, that's not going to change unless you act. You can't expect everything to keep going the way it has and for you to miraculously become happier or attract the things you want. It takes work, and it takes courage to get past your fear of the unknown and claim the life you want. But it is worth it.

Once you push through that, you will discover that you deserve a better life and a greater life that makes you happy. Happiness starts with inner peace. It also starts with learning to forgive yourself for everything that's happened and also for not changing it before then. There is absolutely no point making a big, positive change and then indulging in negative thoughts about not making it soon enough.

So learning to forgive yourself is number one – and then you have to forgive everybody else around you. When I started forgiving everybody around me who I felt had caused grief in my life, all the things that I was asking for started to come to me.

* * *

I still struggle with patience – I probably always will – but I don't struggle with who I am, and that's the difference. I still have those everyday battles that most human beings have, but I have the tools and the knowledge to clear them out very quickly and to reaffirm my mindset. Every human being knows when they're starting to lag or they're starting to feel down or starting to feel like negativity is creeping in, and it requires vigilance – and some practice – to be able to combat it.

When I am working on manifesting something, I don't tell anybody what I'm doing – no one at all.

That's because any negativity or input from someone who doesn't understand how the universe works is negativity that I don't need – and you don't need it either. For example, you might say, 'I want to buy the ten-storey hotel over there' – but you're not saying it out of ego, because you really want that hotel to be able to put sick kids there, to help a charity; whatever it may be. Somebody else may hear that and scoff at it and laugh at it, and that single moment of energy can make you doubt what you're asking for, and their negative thoughts are also put into the universe and can affect what you're manifesting. So I never tell anybody what I'm manifesting or what I'm looking to create, at all, ever, until I have it and then I'll show you.

At the time I was going through my turmoil and screaming at the gods, I was helping my parents out financially – not helping them out with paying the bills, but if they needed help I would be there because my dad was still sending half of his wage over to Croatia. I had some financial commitments of my own – I had purchased a property when I was younger and I was trying to pay that off. I also had plans to go overseas, to Croatia.

I said to the angels, 'Why is it that I'm driving this Ford Capri? The windows won't go up and it's forty degrees!' I said, 'You're telling me to have faith – where's the faith in me not having any money to be able to pay for my windows to be fixed? This car is stuffed!'

I was crying because I was so frustrated. I felt like I was always doing the right thing by people so why was this happening to me? I'd listened to my parents, I'd been a good girl, so why was I struggling? I was banging the steering wheel and swearing at the angels and everybody else.

In my head I heard the message that abundance comes to those who wait and who have faith. But my response was: 'Oh, all right. Have faith! I've been having faith all right, with a car that isn't working and I'm boiling and sweating my arse off.'

The other thing I heard was to give money to charity; that was very clear too.

One day I drove to Sydney for some reason – I can't remember why – and while I was parked by the side of the road this guy tapped on my window asking for money.

I looked at him and said, 'I've got no money.'

He said, 'Yes, you do, you can give me fifty dollars.' I actually can't remember the exact amount, but he was showing me this prayer card and saying, 'There are great things coming for you. You're going to be so filthy rich, you're going to be so rich that you're not even going to know what's happened.' And I'd like to make the point here that for me 'rich' isn't only financial – it refers to relationships, health and family. It's being filthy rich in abundance, and manifesting everything we want in life.

This was the time when things were starting to happen for me spiritually in a really big way. But despite yelling at the universe and hearing the message about abundance and charity, in that moment I wasn't putting two and two together. So I kept saying to this guy, 'I have no money to give you.' I'd spent some money to get my hair blow dried because I was going out – you might think it wasn't the best reason to not have spare money to give him, but that's what it was.

He persisted, saying, 'You're going to give me the money, because you can afford to give me the money, and you know that those who have faith in God will be rewarded by their faith.'

He walked off, then he came back and tapped on the window again. I felt so bad that I didn't have money to give him that I said, 'Can't you come back next week? I can come back down to Sydney. I get paid in two weeks.'

'No,' he said, 'you can't come back because I won't be here. I need this money now – we need to help people.'

I thought, *You're just going to put this money in your pocket and you are going God knows where, and it's my money you're going to take and you're offering me a prayer card.*

He pointed to the photo on the card and said, 'See this person?' The person on the card was a spiritual figure like the Dalai Lama who talked about peace and awareness and those sorts of things.

'I don't know who this is,' I said.

'Well, you need to give money,' he said. He wanted me to help him.

Something inside of me changed, although I have no idea why – we all have those moments, don't we, when something 'clicks'? Right then my thoughts changed to: *I've got to give this man the money.*

I only had about forty dollars in my wallet, so I said, 'I'll give you thirty.'

He said, 'No, no, give me all of it.'

I said, 'I've got maybe twenty-five bucks in my bank account to get home,' and if I gave him all my money, I would not be going out that night.

But I gave him everything I had, including the last coins in my wallet. Afterwards, I couldn't believe I did it. And I couldn't hang around in Sydney with no money, so I drove back to Newcastle. That's when everything started to unfold.

Before this happened I had visualised myself having a beautiful car – a Porsche or a Mercedes – because I was reading the book *Divine Guidance* by Doreen Virtue, learning how to differentiate true guidance from false guidance, and that one of the arts of manifestation is that you actually have to smell, speak and feel something into existence. If it's a car you want, that means you feel the interior, you smell the scent, you feel yourself driving it, you're acting as if you've already received it.

So I'm driving home, screaming at the universe after giving my money away and getting this little prayer card, saying, 'I've given my money – now what?' I don't always get an answer – sometimes I just see flashes of blue lights, and I know that's my angels, it's Archangel Michael, who I speak to all the time.

As I was driving the Capri I was visualising myself in a different car, saying, 'This is amazing – I'm getting my new Porsche and I'm getting my new Mercedes and I'm driving this car and it's so amazing.' Then I'd snap out of it for a minute and say, 'It's so amazing, the windows won't wind up!' So I'd be tapping in and out of my consciousness. I swear those beings up there have a right old laugh at me when I do something like that.

There are times when I keep my faith but then I'd be angry again, so I wasn't keeping my faith. Just because I know what I'm *meant* to do, that doesn't mean I always do it. It's like anything: we know that we're meant to eat healthily but how many of us do it all the time? So when I tell you about how I manifest things, it's not me saying, 'I'm perfect at it and you should be too' – what I'm saying is, 'I'm not always consistent, I don't always keep the faith, because I'm human – and you are too. So if I can manifest things, you can do it as well.'

A year or so after I gave money to that man, I was sitting in a Porsche – *my* Porsche. I had visualised that into my existence. I didn't want that car out of ego – it was about realising I was worth my dream car. I like the way those cars look and feel, their quality and, like a pink diamond, it was a manifestation of hard work and focus. And I deserved this car: I was helping other people, giving money to charity when I was doing my readings at Angels on the Lake, so why shouldn't I have a Porsche if that's what I choose to have? We all have symbols that mean something to us – they can be physical, for you it might be a certain type of handbag, or a house – or they can be a feeling, like being safe or loved.

Some people might think I should just give to other people and not expect anything for myself, but that's

not balanced. If you just give, give, give all the time –
as so many people do – with nothing coming back in,
you end up empty. And once you're empty, you can't
give any more. If you want to have a life where you
can give to other people because you want to, you also
need to be able to receive. It's about balance, and it's
about asking for things in a mindful way. That means
you can't take, take, take either, because that also burns
you out – think of people you know who take all the
time and don't give. They are probably never going to be
satisfied with what they have. Nothing is ever going to
be enough. They're probably not shining it up ...

There was another time when I was still depressed
about the break-up of my relationship and I had written
a list of what I wanted in a new relationship. In my
mind's eye I saw images of what was going to happen.
I saw images of other people's lives. I'd close my eyes
and see images of people. When I was asking my angels
about my relationship, I'd say, 'All right, what is it that
I need to know about my soulmate?' I could never see
the face of the person in my mind's eye, but I used to
ask, 'Show me the man I'm going to marry.' I'd see me
dancing with him, but all I could see of him was longish
hair. The angels always showed me the back of him
and I used to get so pissed off. I'd say, 'Why are you

showing me everything about everybody else but you won't show me how he looks?' I was being taught a lesson in patience.

I won out, though – eventually. As I've said, I'm still working on being patient with most things, so this was no exception. Patience rewards you with the things you ask for; patience brings you what you want at the precise time it is meant to happen. And it's not on my time, it's not on your time, it's on the universe's time. The universe knows the perfect timing – not me. I don't know the perfect timing. Neither do you. There are synchronised events that reveal what's really going on.

Many human beings think, *What I want has to happen right now because it's perfect timing for* me – but it's not necessarily perfect timing for the highest good or perfect for how it's going to affect everybody around you. Part of being patient is trusting that things will happen for you in the right time and the right way *but it's not for you to determine that*. What's good for you has to be for the good of all, and it's that second part that can seem hard to understand. I haven't always been patient about things – remember I was banging on that Capri steering wheel? – but I know that everything has happened with perfect timing, even if it wasn't what I decided was the right time.

So every day I'd see this person in my mind's eye – it's just images, like in a movie theatre, going past, of things that were happening. But the angels never showed me the face. I had to wait to see it, in person, in the future.

* * *

People have said to me, 'You're my guru.' Actually, you are your own guru! I don't want to see you for a reading again for another year and a half, so I won't be in your life every day giving you guidance. I'm just able to hear the messages that you're supposed to hear at the time you come to me. You can do it too – I firmly, truly believe that. But my messages are much clearer because I have complete faith in what I hear from your spirit guides.

So I'm nobody's guru. The only guru you have is yourself, and you need to connect inwards to hear that. Many people I see for a reading will say, 'I just want to come back to you every six months.' Or they say, 'You charge so much for a psychic reading.' I charge what I charge because I know my self-worth. If I think with a poverty-consciousness state of mind, I'm going to receive that. I don't care what you think, because if I did care what you think, I wouldn't be able to tell you what your angels need you to hear or create the bigger purpose of what I want. I wouldn't be able to create the abundance of the things I'm asking for – and that is abundance of love, health, happiness, all sorts of things – so I can help other people on a much bigger scale. If I want to live a particular lifestyle, I can choose to live it, and I choose to do that because that's in my highest good and if I'm in my highest good I'm better able to help other people.

What I am going to tell you, though, is that *you can create the same thing.* Why aren't you asking for that? Because you don't know your self-worth or you feel guilty or fearful of what others might think. I have been at that point and I followed my intuition to change my life. And I am proud of that. I'm not going to lower my expectations because you're not happy about what I'm asking for.

I don't have a poverty-consciousness way of thinking – and by that I don't just mean financial poverty. We can feel poor in health and relationships, or in spirituality. I used to think like that. But I never will again. And that was a state of awareness that I needed to learn in life, in order to evolve. I believe that every single human being has unlimited abundance – you just need to know how to tap into it, and you have to consistently practise manifesting and be aware of your state of mind.

I used to drive my car and look out the window at people and say, 'I bless you with abundance,' 'I bless you with success,' 'I bless you with a debt-free life.' And I really felt it when I was saying it. I truly believed it with my whole being. And every time I walked past someone who was asking for donations, I'd give my money, and I'd continually give without wanting to receive back. I just thought, *Everyone is abundant*.

However, there have been times when I've wavered in that faith, or dropped it, and then things would happen in my life where I wouldn't quite know what was coming next, but I only had to raise my vibrations again for things to get better. The important thing in life to remember is that by knowing your awareness and knowing your self-worth – in your relationships, your work environment, emotionally, physically, spiritually – that's what's going to take you out of anything tough that you go through.

Financial stress is a challenge for many people. I've had people say to me that I haven't gone through tough times so I don't know what I'm talking about. My oath, I've gone through it! I was living a life where I was completely in debt, helping my parents, couldn't pay the bills, driving a car that wouldn't work, and I used to say to the angels, 'What are you doing to me? Where are you guys? You're telling me to be abundant! I'm poor right now!' And then I'd have to change my mindset and say, 'No, I'm actually not poor. I'm wealthy, successful and abundant, and I am collectively, universally rich,' and give gratitude for the positive things I have in that moment. My thoughts create my experiences. *Your* thoughts create *your* experiences.

It's important to realise that nobody is more wealthy and abundant than anyone else, it's just that their vibrational energies have risen and have been able to stay that way. But if somebody has created wealth through a fraudulent activity, or through manipulating an event, they will not keep that wealth, they will not keep that power.

There were a lot of times when I'd be envious of people who had nice things, and I'd say, 'Why is it that they've got that and I can't have that?' Or they had a loving relationship and I wanted that. Then I started realising that I actually *can* have that. If I want that, I can have that. But I have to want it with the right intent. If I want something – a particular pair of shoes, for example – just because I want other people to see me in those shoes, that's not the right intent. If I want those shoes, however, because they're beautifully made and I know I'll wear them for years, and I like how they look on my feet, that's a different intent.

When I believed I had nothing – I had all this debt, I felt like my life was going nowhere – consciously I thought, *You must tell yourself that you're successful and feel and act as if you have already received that.* But I used to wonder, *How do I do that when I don't even have a cent in my pocket and no idea of how to get my life back together?* The answer was simple: I needed to give gratitude. Keep your vibrations up by giving thanks that you're healthy, that your body works, that you have a place to live, that there is music to listen to, that the sun is shining, that you have food to eat. Most of us have many things to be thankful for if only we'd be more conscious of them.

There is an exchange of energy that happens when we practise acts of gratitude and kindness. When someone asks you for money, give them your last cent because that act of faith means that the universe will respond. Know that you're worthy of whatever another person has and be thankful of everything good in your life and the qualities you have.

I'm going to use an example involving money because I think we can all relate to that. When I started doing readings, the cost was fifteen dollars an hour. And at this time I was booked out for a month. Six months later, I said, 'Okay, I'm going to raise my fee to sixty dollars.' And the response was, 'It's a bit expensive.' No, it wasn't! Then I raised it again – I was making a statement about asking for what I was worth. And by this time people were saying, 'You can't do that.' And I told myself, 'Yes, I can! Because my intuition said that I could!' People don't know that I was giving half of that money to charity – I don't need to tell anyone what I do with my money. If you do that, what you're really trying to do is prove to other people that it's okay for you to charge what you charge so you don't feel as guilty for asking for what you're worth. *That* is a poverty-stricken mindset.

So I kept increasing my rate. I deserve this money because I know I give a service that is worthy of what I'm asking for and, on top of that, I know what my self-worth is. Why should I only receive twenty-five dollars an hour, when I know my self-worth? If you don't want to pay that, you don't have to. But I'm not going to allow you to tell me I'm charging too much, or use manipulative arguments such as, 'You shouldn't be charging for the sort of work you do.' Usually that's said by people who haven't worked out their own self-worth, so they try to challenge mine by saying that what I do isn't 'work' because I'm drawing on something innate and I should give it away. Think of when you go to a movie: you don't question how much the actors were paid for their roles because you value their work and what they're providing you with. Similarly, I'm doing work for other people and it brings value to them.

So when someone has a crack at me for charging for readings, all I can see is someone who isn't sure that they're worth whatever they're being paid for their job, or someone who believes that what I do is easy and they wish that they could have 'easy' work too. These people are usually so stuck on what other people have – thinking about it, being envious of it – that they can't attract what they want and they haven't found what they're passionate about, so they can't direct their life towards that. They don't believe that they can have the life they want because they don't believe that they're worth it.

That could be because of how they've been brought up – I think we all know people who have a hard time developing self-worth, and maybe you are in that situation too. Every day, in the media, on social media, we are given a lot of messages about how many things we need to fix and change about ourselves. Or maybe they've found themselves in a situation where their sense of self-worth dissolved, as mine did at one time, and they haven't been able to build it up again.

Sometimes it's easier to look at someone who knows their self-worth and think he or she is egotistical or up himself or herself or whatever it is – but that doesn't do you any good. That thought doesn't touch the person who has self-worth; the only person it affects is you, because you're thinking negatively about someone else and those negative thoughts are toxic.

When I realised my self-worth, I could stand confidently in it. What I want for *everyone* – for you, for me, for the whole world – is for them to know their worth and *ask for what they're worth* in all situations. Because if you don't know your self-worth, it means you're letting other people decide what it is for you. And why would you want to do that?

Never make apologies for what you ask for in life if you do it with the right intent. But if you ask for money because you just want to be sitting by yourself up on the hill, and having servants serve you, that's not the right intent. I knew a woman who married a man for money; you might know someone like that too. Often, women who make that kind of decision aren't yet aware of their self-worth. I said to her, 'Why are you marrying this dude? He's not that nice to you and he's an alcoholic, and just because he sold a business for millions of dollars, what is that going to do for you if you're living in a mansion with this man who treats you badly? What is his house going to do for you?' After they married, he lost all that money. So the universe spun that quickly around for him and now he doesn't have the house, he doesn't have the money. He might have one sports car left. All his money is gone, his abundance is gone, because he didn't help people. He kept it all for himself, and he didn't want to help anybody else. He wanted everybody to say, 'Look at you, you're so amazing, you're so wealthy, you are somebody in society.' But you're nobody in society, because everybody in society is on the same level. After all that, he was abusive towards her too, and she's no longer with him. If she had known her self-worth, though, I highly doubt she would have found herself in that situation in the first place.

It's important to know that we are all inherently worthy, and I see everyone as being on one level. I think it's really interesting that people judge other people according to what they have – 'oh, they have a nice house', 'she has nice jewellery', 'he has an expensive car'.

Things don't make a person. I use my vision board, and if I want a house at the beach and I put that on my vision board, I'm going to have that house at the beach. But that house doesn't define who I am. It is just a manifestation of my sense of self-worth – but not what

I should be judged on. I remember walking up a hill in a beautiful beachside suburb of Newcastle, saying, 'God, where am I going to live?' And God said, 'You're going to live here' – and my attention was drawn to a particular house. Before that I used to dream that I was living by the beach, and I couldn't quite grasp what I was being shown but I knew my haven was manifesting. I was going to have a house on the beach because I need to look over water. I am a creator and a manifestor and I deal with a lot of people's energy, which means I need to be in a place that can balance all of that. The water does that, and it calms me as well. So my mindset then was that I'm going to have a house on the beach, and I'm going to be known in whatever it is I choose to do because being known publicly will allow me to help more people. That was my mindset. And I believe that is my higher calling.

Even with all the experiences I'd had, though, and what I know about how the universe works, when I looked at that house I thought, *There's no way I'm ever going to live there*. But the universe said, *You will be living there*.

Six months later I was living in a house in front of the beach. Just like all the things on my vision boards, I had manifested that lifestyle. And the point of the story is that I will receive wonderful things into my life because I know that's what I'm worthy of. And tomorrow, if I want to say to myself, 'I want to be making a hundred million dollars a year,' that's my right. Just like it's your right and everybody else's right. But some people don't see that possibility – that potential; they just see what's going on in their lives at this very moment and they can't get out of that state of consciousness so there can be no expansion or change. I think this is where I come in, with my work.

The positive manifestations in my life aren't only physical acquisitions like a car or a house. Good health, love, a strong relationship – these are all very important things that I have worked hard to create for myself. I know that hardships come for us all but having the tools to fight against negativity is just as important as self-worth. And those are lessons I am still constantly learning.

I know that I have gone through certain adversities in order to be able to connect with people. I come from a family where I never, ever saw certain life problems, but I have experienced things since that have helped me understand the people I work with better. I never saw anybody in my family have affairs. But I've experienced this. As I've done readings, I've seen people have affairs and I've thought, *This is outrageous!* But I've been primed to tell myself, *All this shit happens in life, but you need to come and connect when you give these readings. These things are happening in everyday life to people and they think they can't get out of the situation. They don't know their self-worth.*

I believe most people won't develop their self-worth or go for what they want because they think it's all too hard. It's easier to be in that state of anger or frustration about what's wrong in their life. It's actually easier to be angry than it is to be happy, because when you're happy you have to take responsibility for what's going on. But if you're angry all the time, you're in that state of consciousness where you don't have to acknowledge what's really happening and the choices you made to get yourself there. Many women and men will float along like that until they get to a point where they say to themselves, 'Well, actually I'm not happy. What do I do now? Where do I go from here?' The truth is always inside you, and that's the place to go to for answers. It takes work, and practice, to connect with yourself, but you can start that conversation today.

And there is the flipside of that. When you're happy, you need to acknowledge why you're happy and why these good things are happening for you, and also acknowledge the things you don't want in your life. The cycle of gratitude never ends – and why would we want it to? Each day you can find at least one thing to be grateful for: the sun is shining, or you see a beautiful tree on your way to work. It doesn't take a lot of time or effort to express gratitude for that. Little by little, you will start to realise that you have a lot to be thankful for – even if you thought you didn't – and then that will make you assess yourself and your life differently. From that your feeling of self-worth grows – and once you have that, there are so many possibilities ahead of you.

Being authentic

After reading what I've said about psychic abilities and manifesting what you want in life, you may still be saying, 'Yes, Jackie, that's all well and good – but I *do not know where to start!*'

Or maybe you're thinking, *I know what you're telling me but I feel so out of control of my life that I just don't know what to do next.* You're not alone in that: we all have times when we feel like no matter what we do, life just isn't going the way we want it to. It feels like someone else is driving your car and you're not going to a desirable destination. As I've said, I understand because I've been in that situation myself.

But I had to show you what was possible before I could get to the fundamentals of what you need in order to make this possible in your life. It's important for you to know that you do have power to change your situation if you want to. If you find yourself in a situation you don't want to be in, you can change it.

I'm not a psychologist but I know how to read energy. The only way to move forward out of whatever you're going through is by recognising that something isn't working in your life and you must change it. This means looking at your life if you're not happy. You might have to change your surroundings, or shift your work. Whatever it is, you need to acknowledge it and you need to take responsibility for what needs to be done. I didn't want to acknowledge that my relationship with Paul was going the way it was going because I created that. It was nobody else's fault, not even that man's – *I did it*. I'm the only person who has power over me. But I lived in fear of losing that relationship because I thought this was the guy I was going to marry.

But when that relationship was falling apart and I yelled at the universe, it was like I was watching a movie – I could see it all in my mind's eye. The universe showed every time that man misbehaved. I thought I was losing it, but I was not; I was seeing images of things that had happened.

The next day I went to Paul and cried and said, 'I know every time you've ever misbehaved.'

The first thing he said was, 'What friend of mine told you?' And then he confessed and he cried.

So that was the authentic truth about him. He had misbehaved. But I wasn't being authentic at that time either – I was out partying with my friends and not listening to my intuition. I didn't want to acknowledge that I was unhappy. It was easier to party than acknowledge that I was in a bad place and make changes.

I'm telling you this because I know, for sure, that I am not the only person who has done this. You probably know someone right now who is staying in a terrible relationship because they just don't want to end it. They don't want to admit that it's terrible, perhaps, or they don't want to be alone. Maybe that's you. Here's the thing: by denying what is going on, by not being true to your authentic self about what you want in your life and why your current situation is something you do not want, the relationship is not going to change. Your level of happiness is not going to change. Do you know anyone who has been genuinely miserable in a relationship and then everything has changed and suddenly the relationship is all wonderful? I don't. There are people who might act as if it's all great but that's them not being genuine. Sure, relationships are fixable if both parties are willing to be honest and authentic about everything, but it has to be about everything going on in the relationship. Presenting one story to the world while there's another story going on at home is not authenticity. Pretending is not going to get anyone anywhere good. Only when you are being authentic to who you truly are and what you truly want will you be able to have the life that's meant for you.

These days it's so easy to be aware of other people's lives and values, or lack of them – or the impression someone is trying to give – because it's all on display. And people are struggling. I get a real sense that people are struggling to be who they are. In some ways we are freer to be who we are than we were a generation ago, but we're more constrained by expectations. I think that comes down to social media and television. Over the past fourteen years of giving readings, I have noticed that there is so much anxiety in people and I believe it's because everything is instantaneous. The birth of social media, I believe, has heightened it because of unrealistic expectations. There is no slow time. There is no communication. There's only who looks good, who looks amazing. *I have the best ring, I have the picture-perfect relationship, I have to show everybody, I am competing with the next person, I am better than that person, I have a better job, I have more money.* So many people are trying to live through appearances, through external happiness rather than internal.

A friend said to me once when we were out in Sydney, 'You know why everyone takes so many drugs? Everyone goes, goes, goes and by the time it gets to Friday night or Saturday, all they want to do is unleash because they're so busy in their life, in their jobs, they don't have any other life.' And these days, that exhaustion is exacerbated by social media. Because so many people are trying to look good. Because many people want to display the fact they have nice things. But what is it doing to you as a person? Is it allowing you to live a fulfilled life? Or to live a life that looks good to someone else but is not good for you, and then it causes all these other emotions to come up? You may get filler in your lips even though you don't necessarily want it or need it, but you're going to do it anyway because you think you'll look good to the guy you're trying to attract. Even saying that is giving me a headache.

You can remove yourself from that pressure by loving who you are, because loving who you are is being authentic to yourself. It's choosing the things that make you happy and knowing that you are enough.

So many women say to me, 'I just want to be married and I want to have children.' I thought like that and it meant I stayed in a toxic relationship. It takes work to change your outlook but it is worth it. Now, I tell them I'd prefer to hug myself at night. I don't need a man to make me happy. And they say, 'How can you be like that?' I can say that because I've been in that place of waking up every morning looking at somebody who made me feel so bad. Being with a man just for the sake of it, or out of ego, is not authentic for me.

I've done readings with men and they're already testing me and I know it because I'm already being told by spirit, *All right, you knew this was going to happen.* The man might be having an affair, and I can see it. But I don't judge him – I'm just going to give him what I hear from the other side. I'm impartial, I'm an instrument. But then I'll say to the man, 'You had an intuition that your relationship wasn't going to last and you walked down the aisle with her anyway – why did you do it?'

Sometimes the answer is something like, 'Because I thought it was the right thing to do – she was pregnant.'

'So why are you still in it when you're arguing every day and your children see that?' I'll ask. 'That's worse. Your children already know that this is not a loving environment, but you're still sitting there because you don't want to lose money by divorcing her.'

The man who does that isn't being authentic and it will only cause suffering for other people in his life – and for himself. This also applies to women who do things that aren't authentic.

People are desperate for connection with other people but at the same time, because there's this competitiveness going on, it's almost like other people are the enemy. So much of that is because we're so aware of what other people are doing, due to social media and websites. I've been there. I think we've all been there. You feel insecure, you don't know your self-worth, so you measure yourself against other people. I've realised in life that if you don't have a connection with yourself, if you don't love who you are, you can't take responsibility for the things that aren't working in your life and you're never going to have true happiness. The universe is not going to bring you happiness unless you're happy within yourself. When a child's born they're free of any responsibility, they're free to live in the moment. But as soon as they become aware of other people, and the fact that they have thoughts and opinions, that's when everything shifts and life becomes competitive, if they don't love themselves and know their self-worth.

This doesn't mean that I have been 100 per cent true to myself all the time. From the year I started school

I don't think I was ever being true to myself, right up until the time I had the awakening after that relationship with Paul. I wasn't standing up for myself in a loving way. I wasn't being proud of being Croatian born, I felt embarrassed. People had made fun of me for being different. There were times I was nervous about what people were going to think walking past my house with the vegetable garden, and because the house was small and old.

As time went on through school and working in the bank, I wasn't happy; I was just working in a bank because it was good money. I was also hanging around people I thought were being truthful when, deep down in my heart, I knew some of them weren't. I was not speaking up for my beliefs in my working environment, knowing that I deserved more money, deserved more recognition for what I was doing. I was reaching all my targets, but it hardly mattered, because I was in a job I didn't like. I kept going, though I was there out of ego because I knew that it was going to pay the bills and give me a lifestyle that I wanted. There were times that I'd think, *Now I can afford to go and buy that nice whatever*, but was I doing it for myself or was I doing it to impress other people? I think most of my life at that time was not being truly authentic to me, but I wasn't living my life thinking, *I'm a fake person* – I was living life based on what I knew and what I thought it meant to have a good, successful life.

I had to go to a very dark place in my life to remember who I was. Not to *know* who I was – to *remember*. Because I always knew. When I was a young child, I was authentically me. My parents had instilled values in me that were the pillars of who I was – and who I am today. My dad, for example, taught me to always have respect: respect for myself and for others. He taught me to know that my body is a temple and I have to protect and cherish and nurture it. The confidence I had resonated from that as well. I think confidence is having respect for yourself, because if you don't respect yourself how can you love yourself? Loving yourself is respecting yourself, knowing yourself and living within healthy boundaries.

I forgot those boundaries for a few years, and it took a toll on me. Once I rediscovered my authentic self, though, there were no limits on my life. However, I don't believe that everyone has to go through bad times in order to discover their authentic selves. Those bad times give you a shake-up and a kick up the pants, and say: *Hey, you don't want to end up here again, so what are you going to do about it?* But there are other ways. You absolutely don't need to wait for something big, good or bad to happen to you in order to make this discovery. All you have to do is start wanting it. Start asking yourself questions: *Who am I, really? Who was I when I was a child? What do I want in life?* The thing is, though, you need to be honest in your answers. You can't give answers that you think sound nice or are what someone else wants to hear. Those answers are for you alone to hear.

The answers may not come straightaway. That's okay. Keep asking the questions. And if you need help, ask for that too. Ask your angels, ask the universe, ask God. The help is there for you. But don't stop until you get those answers, because that's how you're going to move on to the next, great stage of your life.

Faith and forgiveness

I was born a Catholic. I've been to church half-a-dozen times in my life. My parents didn't force me to go to church so I didn't. I prayed in my bedroom. My mum always said, 'You can pray to God in your bedroom and God hears you.' I do absolutely believe that there was a Jesus – that there was a prophet. I believe that there were many prophets around the world. And I also believe that we're all prophets – we all have something to say. I believe that God hears all and we are all connected. I believe that faith comes from a higher power that we're all connected to. That higher power for me is all one. My faith comes down to knowing that the highest purpose and the highest good, whatever it is that we're here to do, will be shown to us through learning how to tap into ourselves.

Part of that highest purpose is gratitude – massively. You have to be thankful for the blessings in your life as well as being able to look at all the things that you've done to help people along the way; helping people without wanting anything back.

Faith is believing in the signs that come to you in unexpected ways. It could be from a friend. It could be from a stranger, it could be from a shopkeeper, it could be on TV or in a movie. You may notice something that recurs, like seeing the same number, or seeing feathers or a particular word. That's the universe giving you signs.

Faith is another element in living authentically, and in manifesting what you want in life. It's all very well to have the skills to manifest, but if you don't have faith in the outcome – if you don't have faith in yourself, or believe that you are supported by the universe – you won't get anywhere. It's hard to have faith continually, I get that, because as you can already see, I question things. But I've learnt to have faith, because the support I need is all around me. I've also learnt that my faith is always rewarded.

One of the blockages to having faith is judgement. God does not judge; if you feel judged, it's because you're judging yourself. God doesn't take anything away from you – you're taking things away from yourself by not being authentic or truthful. When someone has had something terrible happen to them because of someone else – someone has hurt them physically or psychologically – people ask, 'Why is this happening? Where is God when this happens?' Yet God never left. Unfortunately that was a decision someone made to hurt another person, and there can be terrible outcomes. It is hard to witness and sometimes it's easier to think that the situation was out of anyone's control – that God did it – but that's not the case: it was in the control of the perpetrator. For the person who is traumatised, it might even seem easier to blame God because if a person is the cause of their pain, they have to deal with the role that person plays in their life.

There's a way to do that, though, because the other side of this behaviour is forgiveness. I believe forgiveness is the great healer. Over the years I have seen so many women and men who are living with high levels of stress or an illness, and often they have a person in their lives they haven't forgiven, someone who has done something truly awful to them. It's as though the stress or illness or disease is their body's way of dealing with that emotional pain – manifesting it physically. I've seen it too many times not to believe it can happen.

That doesn't mean I forgive people for everything they do. I struggle with it at times; I really do. I'm still evolving and I'm still learning to forgive people. And I have to. There are times when there are things going on in my head and I have to check myself and remember to live authentically.

Forgiveness is hard, especially if you have been hurt and you don't want to let go. If you let go of the hurt that means you have to acknowledge what's really going on. And a lot of us – including me, in the past – don't like to do that. It's easier to be a victim, to blame somebody else. The path to healing, to being authentic, to manifesting everything you want in your life, *must* involve forgiveness of others, because otherwise you are leaving a massive road block in your way. That sounds tough, but it's no tougher a road than I've been on myself. Forgiveness is hard work and it takes practice. I know when a negative thought's about to enter and if it does, even if I dwell on it, I only dwell on it for a short time and it's out. If I'm anxious about something, I have to centre myself, calm myself, and I will repeat affirmations over and over and over. It's all about practising gratitude and giving thanks. Exercise helps me too, but it's the positive affirmations that push the thoughts out. That affirmation might be, 'All is well', or

'Everything's happening the way it's supposed to'. If I'm anxious, it might be: 'This is passing', 'This isn't true', 'You *are* in control of you'.

There are a lot of people out there – and this is part of my story as well – who give, give, give, who don't receive anything back and then get upset with other people. It took me so long to realise I shouldn't only be giving with the expectation of receiving something back. You have to give *without* wanting anything back – but you also have to know your self-worth, so you don't get taken advantage of. And the only way to know your self-worth is by not allowing yourself to do things you're not happy with.

Of course, when you're in a marriage or partnership, there are things you have to do that you don't really want to do. But in that situation, it's for the higher good. Maybe you don't feel like going on a date night but you know it's going to make your partner happy – it's for the higher good of your relationship. You're not going to be selfish and not go. When you enter a relationship it's about communication, making sure you create time together and making sure that person knows they're wanted and needed. That doesn't mean you have to stop doing you. If you really, really don't want to go out, don't go out – but work out what's for the highest good, and speak to your partner honestly about how you feel.

Sometimes, I have to say, I have to work on myself. I'm loud and I'm a straight shooter and some people can't handle that. But I'm not going to apologise for who I am. As long as I do everything with the right intent and I'm kind and I'm generous, I'm not going to make apologies. In saying that, I know what is good and what is not good for me as a person. And I want you to learn how to listen to your intuition, because it never lies. If I had listened to my intuition in that relationship with Paul, I would never have gone into it. But I also acknowledge that I have to be thankful for it because it got me back on my path.

Several years ago, when I was going out at night with my friends, wearing myself out, drinking too much and not at all happy about it, I went to a church and lit a candle. I said to myself, 'I'm not going to do that again.' I wasn't going to do things that took me away from who I really was. The things I was doing weren't extreme by most people's standards but the behaviour wasn't true to *me*. I am really not someone who wants to be out all night, every night. I like being at home. I like being with the people I love. I was only doing that because I was trying to get away from *myself* – but, of course, I was always there.

In that church I closed my eyes and saw the image of Archangel Michael with my third eye. I was crying, saying, 'Why did I do this? What was the point of this?' And the answer was: *Do not cry about what you have done – release it, let it go and learn from it, and listen to your intuition.* In other words, I did this to myself. I was hurting myself. I went through all of that because I didn't trust my intuition, something every human being has.

People have said to me, 'You've got the perfect life. You're so positive. You're confident.' Here's the thing – yes, I am confident, because I know who I am and I'm not going to apologise for what I believe in. But it's hard work. There is no such thing as the perfect life. The difference is that I stay committed in my mindset to being positive. I'm always evolving, just like you. You have to go to the same awareness every day in your mind and keep yourself there. You need to have faith. But the only way to stay like that is to surround myself with inspirational people – people who are truthful. People who have my best interests at heart. I already know by looking at somebody if they are truthful, if somebody's spending time with me for the right reasons. I'm very, very big on loyalty. If I'm your mate, I'll be there for you like no other – you're family. But if you're disloyal to me, you're cut. It doesn't mean I dislike you, you're just out of my psyche. I can forgive you but that doesn't mean you need to stay in my life. When I started forgiving myself, forgiving that person in my life who tried to control me, forgiving friends who I believed hurt me, or forgiving the people I was working with, and I released those people from my psyche, that's when I noticed changes in my life.

The bad experiences I've had come down to losing my faith, being angry at God, being angry at the universe, but having something massive happen in my life to bring me back. I told the angels that if I ever go off my path again, they'd better do something. I said that to them when I prayed. I cried and said, 'Take all this negative shit and all the people out of my life who shouldn't be there.' These were people who weren't there for me spiritually or emotionally and who didn't inspire me. They were drainers, and that kind of person is automatically out of my life. I said, 'Take the people out who aren't meant to be in my life; don't do it in a negative way, just take them out.' I haven't had them in my life for many, many years.

Every three months I have a little clean-up, because these people always come into your life, and I always say to my angels, 'If they're meant to be there keep them there; if they're not, take them away.' And I don't do it in a negative way, it's just that these people are going on a different path from me.

It's interesting to see how many people float away from your life when you're on a path that they're not truly comfortable with. But I believe like-minded people who are meant to be there come back into your life because you're attracting them. So many people come for a reading but they don't live their life after the messages that I give them. They either don't weed out the people who are harming them or they don't work to attract and keep the ones who can shine it up with them.

If you are given a message, though, why aren't you going to pay attention to it? This is the universe telling you something important. I yelled at the angels, at God, at the universe, and asked for proof that they were out there. God said, 'All right, I'm going to give it to you, I'm going to show you this angel, show you Archangel Michael. I'm going to give this to you but what are you going to do with it?' I went and did something with it. In my work, I give those messages to other people because I'm the channel for the universe, for the angels. So if I'm giving you a reading and you're given a message, the angels have proved they are there for you – what are you going to do with it? Are you going to carry on as you were? So many people still do the same things that were making them miserable before they came to a reading, and they still don't have faith, even though they've been shown the truth: *We're here!* the angels say. *Ask us for help; we'll help you.* My angels have always said that after every single reading.

I don't attach myself to anybody's energy. I allow them to be who they are, and if they take the advice they're given, if they honour it, they'll move forward. If they don't, then they're going to keep struggling with it for the next however many years until, one day, they *have* to deal with that issue.

After my relationship with Paul I said to the universe, 'If I ever go off my path again, you do something dramatic. I don't care what it is but you need to put me right. Whatever it may be – something might happen in my relationship, in my personal life, in my work. Something might happen with my abundance.' That reminder – that wake-up call – is always going to be something that is going to affect you, where you may lose your faith again and that's going to bring you back, because you created this crisis of faith. You started veering off your path and the universe is bringing you back in.

If I've done something negative, the karma hits me the same day. But when I'm asking something, it takes a bit longer, because the message is, *You already know.* The reason it gets to me much quicker than most people is because I know the laws of the universe, and when you understand the laws you attract instantaneously. But I can't manipulate the laws because no one can manipulate the laws of the universe.

There are times when I still have to forgive myself for allowing people to hurt me. And there have been times in the last year or two where it has seemed as though people were being disloyal, because I can see there's an element of jealousy in those people. And I ask myself, 'How long have I attracted that?' Situations like that can make me doubt myself, and then I need to practise that forgiveness again.

Every human being has those emotions. You just have to be consistent in dealing with them. Really, the only thing you need to be concerned with is yourself and being consistent with being kind and loving to you. Everything else has to flow from that – it's just not possible to move on to a bigger, brighter life without it.

The triumph of love

I haven't said a lot about my sister, but that's not because she's an unimportant part of my life – she is. She's had a lot of ups and downs, too, and just as there are parts of my story that you may relate to, parts of hers could resonate for you too. They certainly do for me, because I love her and care about her.

One day when I was thirteen years old I was on a bus, returning home, and I remember feeling anxious. When I got home I saw ambulances out the front and the first thing I thought was that they were there for someone in my family. Dad was at work and Mum was just finishing her shift at the Newcastle Workers Club; there were days when we'd come home and it was fine for us to be by ourselves until four-thirty or five o'clock. My brother Bobby and I were both teenagers, so we were responsible enough to be home without parents and to look after Angela, who was ten at the time.

As I arrived home my next-door neighbour came over to me. I started to cry straightaway, thinking that something terrible must have happened to a member of my family. And there was Angela, in the back of the ambulance. Our neighbour was in the ambulance with her.

My sister had been riding her bike without a helmet down our steep driveway, then she swung out onto the road and a car hit her. She fell off the bike and smacked the side of her head on the concrete. When I saw her my first thought was, *Is she dead?*

Thank God she wasn't, and as soon as Mum came home we drove straight to the hospital. Mum said she had a feeling that day that something was going to happen – she didn't know what it was, she just had this feeling that she had to get home.

Angela could have died – the incident was that serious – but she was okay. She had to have her head shaved around the area where her skull split open and she was sewn back together. I felt so sorry for her; I even thought, *Maybe I should stop pulling her hair now ...* And I remember crying and talking to God, saying, 'I love my sister so much and I don't want anything to happen to her.' So often it takes something serious like that to remind us how much we love our family members. That accident reminded me to be a bit nicer and kinder to my sister.

There was another side to that accident, though: Angela received a card from the people who hit her – and then they tried to sue her! I'll never forget that. My mum was working two jobs and my dad was working and they were struggling a little bit, but these people were going to sue anyway because there was a bit of damage to the front of their car.

It was all thrown out of court, but that was such a stressful situation for my parents: Angela nearly died and nothing happened to the other people apart from a dent in their car.

I was always very strict with Angela, even when she got older, about where she was or what she was doing, even when she was fifteen and sixteen. 'What are you up to?' I'd ask, because sometimes it felt like she was testing us: she'd say she was somewhere but I didn't believe her. I would also have to take her everywhere I went. If I was planning to go out, my dad would say, 'You've got to take your sister.' Or she'd scream if she wasn't allowed to come, so I had to take her, otherwise I wasn't allowed to go.

As we got older Angela would say, 'You're always judging me – you always have to know where I am and what's going on. Why? *Why?*' But she would never tell me anything. I had a feeling that she was going out a lot and not focusing on her studies – she was supposed to be in Sydney studying, but she was failing some subjects. I drove to Sydney because I wanted to keep an eye on her. When I arrived I said, 'I'm staying with you' – but she wouldn't let me stay in her apartment, so I couldn't keep as close an eye on her as I'd planned.

It was a phase, of course: she's now an emergency department nurse with all the responsibility that it brings. I don't think I was wrong to be the concerned big sister, though – I'll always want the best for her.

When Angela told me she was dating this guy who I will call Derek, I saw a flash in my head of him being physically abusive. I said to her, 'You can't be with him. He's going to hit you.'

She said, 'You're just jealous!'

But I knew what I'd seen. 'He's going to hit you, Angela,' I said. 'He's not for you.'

She hung up on me.

A while later Angela told my parents that she was going to marry this man. Dad said to him, 'If you ever touch my daughter, there will be consequences.'

Derek's response was: 'I don't know what you're talking about. I would never do that.'

But my dad had a feeling about it all – he'd obviously seen something, just as I had.

When I met Derek for the first time, he couldn't really look at me. A few weeks later, after I'd met him again, he had the hide to say to my sister that I'd changed what I was wearing three times because I wanted him to look at me. He was trying to fabricate a revolting story: *Your sister wants me.* Obviously that is a twisted thing to do, but that was probably his way of trying to make Angela not believe what I had told her. Therefore, my first impression was that he was a mean, nasty, horrible person.

My reservations weren't going to stop the wedding going ahead, though. Angela and Derek were married in a church and the ceremony included some traditions unfamiliar to me: the bride and groom wore crowns and the immediate family members threw lollies and money at the couple. Well, during that part of it, we saw Derek's mother kiss him on the lips. As far as I'm concerned, that's just wrong and weird. So that was one thing. Then, as his mother was throwing coins at my sister as she and Derek were walking around the church, Angela's crown fell off. At that point I just knew that the marriage would be disastrous, especially combined with what I had seen months earlier: that Angela would be with a man who hit her.

Little did I know that he was hitting her before they got married. He'd punch her or kick her where people couldn't usually see. He'd never punch her on the face so we never saw any bruises there, but they were on her legs or her arms.

Sometimes I'd see them, though. I used to say to her, 'What are those bruises from?'

'Oh, shut up, Jackie,' she'd say. 'You don't know what you're talking about.'

When they married, Angela begged me and my husband to help her with a loan to buy a house, because she wanted to move to Newcastle from Wollongong, where she was living. What I didn't know was that she wanted to be close to the family because she was scared, but she was too ashamed to say anything – she confirmed this later on. The reason didn't matter, though, and we agreed to help.

She and her husband bought a house only a few minutes' drive from my parents' place. Angela manipulated that situation – as she needed to – by focusing on what a great house it was. Its proximity to my parents made it easy for my dad to pop in at various times, because he wanted to keep an eye on his daughter. I found out later that Angela was scared the violence would get worse.

After they married, Angela fell pregnant straight-away. I got so angry because I knew her husband wanted her pregnant so she wouldn't leave.

'You haven't even had a honeymoon period with him,' I said to her. 'You don't even know what he's like.'

My reservations didn't mean I wasn't looking forward to meeting my niece or nephew, because no matter how angry I was at Angela's husband, I love her and I would love her child.

When her son Goran was born, my husband and I were there for him, day in and day out. He'd come and stay at our house, even as a baby, for a couple of nights at a time. Angela would allow it because Mum would always say, 'When you have a baby you hand the baby over, otherwise it becomes too clingy.' She's right, and I'll do the same thing when I have children.

So Goran would stay with us for a couple of nights, which I loved and which helped out Angela too because Derek refused to work and insisted that she had to go straight back to work.

I'll be honest: Derek is the one person I struggle to forgive. I pray for everybody but I skip him. What he did to her early in their relationship would be enough of a reason, but it got worse.

One night Angela and Derek were going to a wedding and staying overnight in a rented apartment. Ben and I were babysitting Goran, who was six months old. In the middle of the night, around one o'clock, we got up to feed him. We'd just put him back to bed when Angela called. I saw her name on my phone and thought, *Why is she calling? She's probably having a great night and wants to say hello.* It was so late that I was tempted to not answer the call. I did, though, and she was freaking out.

'I'm trying to call Mum,' she said.

'What's going on?' I said – then she hung up.

She called my parents' house next and my mother answered the phone. When Dad walked out to see what was going on Mum was standing there holding the phone, and she'd gone white.

My sister had told her that she was in a cupboard, pushing against the door with her feet, because Derek was trying to pull her out by her hair. He had punched her in the face repeatedly with a closed fist. Derek had trained as a fighter.

Angela was an hour and ten minutes' drive away from Mum and Dad that night. My parents got in the car and were there in forty-five minutes. Dad flew, Mum said later. Meanwhile Mum was on the phone to Angela, who was screaming, 'Help me, Mum! Help me, Mum! I'm in the cupboard. He's trying to get in! He's trying to get me!'

Derek was drunk, which no doubt made things worse. And as he got her out of the cupboard, he pinned her down and punched her repeatedly, and she heard somebody in her head say, *Grab his balls, twist and push up.* So Angela grabbed his balls and she twisted and she pushed them up, just like she was told.

That got him to stop long enough for her to run out of the room, and she fled downstairs in her pyjamas. Then she was out on the road, crying and in shock, while her husband was throwing full bottles of beer at her from the balcony.

A woman came out of the building to see if she could help but my sister screamed at her to go away. Angela obviously wasn't thinking straight – how could she? How does anyone know how to deal with something like that? If you've never been in that kind of situation it's hard to understand, but my sister's first instinct would have been survival, and she acted accordingly.

By that time Angela was on the phone to Ben, and Mum was on the phone to me. Angela managed to get to the nearest police station, and we'd already rung them. She was sitting in that police station having been pummelled to within an inch of her life by her husband – and then she started protecting him. What I'd seen, all those months before when I told her that she would be with a man who hit her, was this moment, her sitting in the police station.

'It was my fault,' she said. 'I shouldn't have done what I did. I shouldn't have told him he had to get up off the floor and get to bed because it's my birthday tomorrow.'

She started to think about what Bobby and Dad would do if they found out the extent of what Derek had done to her. 'You don't know my dad,' she said to the police. 'If my dad sees me like this, he's going to lose it. You're going to have to try to control my dad.'

All of this was Angela trying to work out how to protect her husband, who had just punched her over and over again and dragged her out of a cupboard by her hair.

As it turned out, one of the police officers had known me for years, so that gave my sister some sense of safety. They were trying to calm her down, trying to think of other things to talk about to distract her, and then Angela started saying again, 'You don't know my dad. You don't know my brother.' She was worried about what they would do to Derek.

At this time it had been a few months since I'd spoken to Bobby. A lot of siblings go through patches where they don't get on, and in our family it's no different. But this is where family loyalty comes in. He was living in a different state then. I rang him three times that night before he answered.

'Our sister's been bashed,' I said, 'and you have to get here.'

'What?' Bobby said. He had only met Derek a handful of times.

'Our sister's been hit,' I repeated.

My brother got in his car and drove all night, to be with Angela.

Meanwhile, Derek was still in the apartment. The police arrested him and charged him (later, he was convicted of assault). As they were walking him into the police station my father arrived, and he lunged at Derek.

The cops grabbed Dad and said, 'Please don't do anything. Just calm down.'

The next day, my sister put sunglasses on and wouldn't take them off, because her face puffed up like a cauliflower. By then Bobby had arrived. He pulled the glasses off her face, and a tear slid down his cheek. But this was the turning point for Angela. This was the reckoning. Her life and her worth were more important than staying in this marriage, yet even after everything that had happened she was still making excuses for Derek.

Mum asked if I could see what would happen to them.

'She's going back one more time to see him,' I said. 'But that's going to be the moment when I step in.'

'She wouldn't do that,' Mum said.

But she did. My sister went back to him one more time. I don't know what she was looking for. Maybe she wanted to find reasons where there were none. She believed he still loved her.

I called Angela and I said, 'If you go back to him I will use every resource I have to make it known that you're an unfit mother. I'm the godmother of that child, my Goran, and Ben is his godfather, and I will do that to protect him.' I know how that sounds: tough. Very, very tough. But I was not going to allow Goran to be put in harm's way. Plus I wanted Angela to wake up and see what she was doing. She was making excuses for a violent man because she felt she deserved his violence, but she did not. She never did. *No one ever does.*

'You can't do that!' she said.

'You watch me,' I replied. 'I will.'

What I said gave her something to think about but she made up her own mind not to go back to him.

Angela's path has not been easy but she made it out. If there was something good to come out of that experience, it's that she can have no doubt that her family loves her and loves her son. We were raised to be loyal, and loyalty came through that night and in the days and years that followed. Sometimes we have to say hard things to the people we love to shake them out of beliefs that are damaging. That's what I had to do for my sister. But it was done out of love. I wanted her to realise that she was worth so much more than being a punching bag. I wanted her to love herself the way we loved her. I still want that for everyone I love.

Now she's free, and our beautiful Goran is a happy little boy.

Finding my soulmate

We're all looking for a soulmate. A true love. I was, for a long time, and so often the people I meet through my work are looking for love. My husband, Ben, is the soulmate I prayed for, and I am his.

You know when a person is meant for you. They're not just there for the coin, or for the status, or because they don't want to be alone or they just want to be married: they're there because they love you unconditionally, and they will do whatever they have to in order to make sure that you are happy as well.

That doesn't mean that they control your happiness – it means they *enhance* it. You come together as a team. You allow each other to be who you are, and you don't make judgements about things each of you do.

I know the worst of the worst about my husband, he knows the worst of the worst about me, and we don't judge each other about any of it. And I know what it's like to not have that. With my first major relationship I felt like love was conditional. With Ben, I know there are no conditions, ever.

* * *

When I was thirteen I shared a bedroom with Angela. We had bunk beds and I had the top one. I had all these posters everywhere: Michael Jackson, New Kids on The Block, Girlfriend, Justin Timberlake – all the hotties back in the day, according to me. Apparently I also had a Silverchair poster but I actually don't remember putting it up – it was my sister who reminded me of it years later.

I might have had rock stars on the walls but I also had a blue bedspread covered in Care Bears. I loved that bedspread; I didn't want to get rid of it, even though I was a teenager. I'd lie on the bedspread looking at the posters and they used to make me feel like an adult. I'd always daydream, sometimes thinking about what it would be like when I was older and married.

Looking back, I believe I was connecting to the other side, connecting to energy. But every time I'd daydream,

my dad would yell out, 'Clean your room!' I didn't feel
so adult after that! So I'd clean the room, and I'd do it
with my sister, quickly, so we could go out and do other
things. I'd shove all my stuff under the bed and in the
cupboard, and I'd tell Dad, 'It's clean – it looks amazing.'
Until one day Dad brought in a rake and raked all this
stuff from under the bed, then opened our window and
threw it out. Our neighbours thought it was the funniest
thing they'd ever seen, but we weren't laughing. Angela
and I were embarrassed and said, 'Stop throwing our
stuff out!'

And Dad said, 'You wanna clean up like this? If this
is how you clean up, it's all going out the window.'

We had to pick it all up and fold up the clothes and
do it nicely.

At first my dad didn't like us having posters up
because he thought they would ruin the walls. Then he
got over it, and said, 'It's your room, but you've got to
keep it clean.' In fact, we had to always keep the whole
house clean in case a visitor turned up. I used to say to
him, 'Why don't you have to clean the house?' and he
never had a good reason.

But back to the point of the story: I had all these
posters and I daydreamed that I wanted to be married
to somebody who was like my prince. I just wanted this

man to sweep me off my feet and I wanted to feel safe in the relationship.

So I'd be visualising that relationship, and I looked at my mum and dad's marriage as an example.

Ben once said to me, 'Do you know what I love about your family? Your dad always wants your mum around, he loves her so much. It's not this controlling thing, it's just really nice.' When Dad has his coffee outside he wants Mum there so he can have a chat with her. When he's doing the gardening he likes having her there so he can chat to her, so she brings out her coffee, and it's all very cute. I love how Mum and Dad are always together, but she still has her independence.

So I wanted to have a man who would sweep me off my feet and put me on the back of his horse and ride away. It's a cliché, and it sounds old fashioned, but that's what I wanted. I even dreamt something like that when I was fourteen or so: I was on a white horse with a man, and he was riding off into the sunset. I couldn't see his face, though; in those sorts of dreams I could never, ever see his face.

When I was in my mid-teens I never looked at guys. I was always the 'frigid' one, always the girl who was quite nervous around boys. Even when I'd go to a party they'd try to talk to me and I wouldn't talk to them, because I knew they'd had a few drinks, and I'd walk off very quickly. After I did my Year Ten School Certificate, out of nowhere came news of this music industry course that was affiliated to Years Eleven and Twelve studies. I was only turning sixteen because I was a year younger than everybody else in my school year – I started school a year earlier than I was meant to.

The music industry course was to be held at a TAFE in Newcastle one day a week. The teacher asked who would like to go and we were given an application form and told that in the course we were going to learn about all the different facets of the industry. At that age I thought I was going to be a dancer or singer or something like that. So the course sounded amazing, and just right for me.

My intuition told me that I was going to be chosen and I was so excited. I told my parents I would be trying out for it because I thought it would help me progress further in the entertainment industry. We had to audition for acceptance to the course, by performing something. I sang, and my song was Tina Turner's 'Simply the Best'. I'd loved singing since I was very young. I used to go to our garage so I could sing with a microphone and an amplifier, which my parents bought when I was about eleven. I would sing every single afternoon with my back-up tapes; I was taking private singing lessons at the time so I needed to practise, quite apart from the fact that I loved to sing anyway. My neighbours used to shout out, 'Shut up, Jackie!' but I wasn't deterred: I would be out in the garage every day singing for hours and hours and hours.

I was accepted into the course, and another girl from the school did it with me. Only a few people from the Hunter region were accepted. The teacher's name was Jane, and I connected with her instantly; I loved her energy. I knew that she loved the music industry and this was where she felt comfortable. It wasn't about having a psychic feeling about her – my psychic abilities didn't come back strongly until I was twenty-three. But I could see this woman was so happy that this course was happening, and maybe my connection with her was because I felt safe doing the course. I felt like I could be who I was, without people judging me. There were about twelve or thirteen students and one of them was this really good-looking guy called Zac. He was a creative and a musician; most of the students were musicians in bands, or they wanted to be in a band.

I remember this guy coming from Sydney and talking to us about how lucky we were that we were participating in this particular course. We were told that we'd be learning about all the facets of the music industry, about recording and sound engineering and producing, and even the business side of it. It was *awesome*.

The man from Sydney had a guitar; he was teaching us about riffs and saying that one of the best songs ever produced in our generation was the Oasis song 'Wonderwall'. I was never into rock music, though: I loved hip hop and R&B. I became a homie – and, to go along with that, I started breakdancing. I taught myself how to do it! In fact, I became a very good breakdancer, if I do say so myself. I taught myself how to pop and lock and how to do my first back spin. It took months, and a whole lot of bruises along the way. I taught myself how to do back spins, helicopters, side flips, everything, and I used to go to Blue Light Discos and battle. And while I was learning all of that I was listening to Eazy-E and NWA ... not Oasis.

So as the guy was teaching us 'Wonderwall' and saying how amazingly produced this song was and how the riff had a hook that connected with people because of its repetition and blah, blah, blah, I was sitting there thinking, *This is all well and good, but a bit boring. I want to know about singing.*

During class they said to us, 'It's such an honour for you to be accepted because there's going to be a very special treat for you next week.'

So that next class we were all sitting there, doing our work, when these three dudes walk in. We looked up – and recognised them. Despite the fact I wasn't a rock chick, of course I'd heard of Silverchair. They were in their prime right then; they'd just been touring with Red Hot Chili Peppers, they'd done their own world tour. This was around the time when girls were camped out the front of their houses.

I'm looking at these three guys thinking I knew them – and that's because they were from Newcastle. Ben, who was the drummer, sat behind me. Dan, the guitarist, also sat behind me. Chris, the bass player, was sitting a little bit further over. They were all besties, and Ben was the smartarse.

I wondered, *Is this the big surprise – these boys? I don't know their music.* The other boys in the class were trying to suck up to Silverchair. A part of me was excited, though, that these boys were in this class. I was a fifteen-year-old girl, after all.

On that first day we had to split up into three groups. I was in Chris's group with a couple of other guys. We all had to come up with some kind of skit or a performance. I sang again – I was so nervous to sing in front of these boys. They had toured the world – they knew what they were doing. I sang the chorus of some

Tina Turner song. I can't remember if it was 'Simply the Best' again, but it probably was, and I was just so embarrassed. I remember them looking at me and all I wanted was to get off the stage.

They kept coming back to class, as students, depending on if they were touring or had other commitments. The course went for a year and a half, so the three boys were in quite a few classes. It turned out that Silverchair were paying for this course to give back to the community and give back to other kids so they could have an opportunity to learn about the music industry. That meant they'd funded my place there, and everyone else's too. But at the time I thought, *So they should anyway because they're out being famous, living the dream – give somebody else the opportunity, thank you very much.*

Ben would sit behind me, always laughing, and always kind of flirting too. *You're such a wanker*, I'd think – only because he was. And, *You think you're so good but you're actually not.* I don't want to say he had an ego but he had so much confidence. He and Dan were always mucking up in class, too. I think Ben was trying to get my attention, but I didn't give him anything because I was being nonchalant towards them. And their smartarsey behaviour turned me off.

Although I have to admit that I could be a smartarse back to Ben. I'd give him a bit of a hard time about things, like what he was eating for lunch. I don't think those guys were used to girls who weren't fawning over them all the time.

After class I'd always stand in a certain spot and wait to be picked up. Because Ben and Dan and Chris didn't have their driver's licences their mums or somebody else would pick them up, so they'd be waiting there too. They'd try to chat with me. Ben had long hair but I didn't think he was that good-looking. I would think, *What's so great about these boys anyway?* even though they were world famous.

As the weeks went on we all became more familiar with each other. When we met again, years later, Ben would say, 'You were the hot chick with the big boobs and confidence,' but I never flirted with them, I'd just talk to them and that would be it.

I had a sixteenth birthday party, and for me and my family the sixteenth birthday is a big thing, so I hired out a hall in Speers Point, I had a DJ, my dad paid for about ten cases of beer and all this alcohol – but the kids weren't allowed to drink unless they had a permission note from their parents. My mum and dad had all their European friends there, and I had all of my friends from high school coming. I even had two security guards. It was full-on. I thought I'd invite the Silverchair boys, because we knew each other fairly well by then, but when I asked them I was so embarrassed. I thought, *They're so not going to come.*

On the day of the party I was really nervous. I had my hair and make-up done; I was wearing a silver dress. Ben, Dan and Chris didn't make it because they were overseas. Some of the other guys from TAFE turned up, though, and I remember all the girls looking at Zac, saying, 'He's so hot.' He was a surfer, with blond hair and olive skin. Years later, when I told Ben that Zac was the hot guy in the course, Ben said, 'He was odd.' I guess everyone forms their own impressions.

To me, Ben stood out more than the other boys in the class. I told my dad the boys from Silverchair were in the course, and about Ben, and he said, 'You're going to marry him one day.' I thought, *Oh whatever, Dad, you might want me to marry him* ... I can assure you that I didn't think of Ben in that way at the time.

The course finished, and I passed – with very good marks. I didn't always get good marks at school, I can tell you. Teachers would always say, 'Jackie talks too much, Jackie doesn't want to listen, but when she applies herself she is very good.' I can get bored with people, and I got bored with the teachers. I was always bored of people taking too long to articulate themselves. *I already know what you're going to say – what's taking you two hours to come out with it? You're doing my head in! I don't have time for this! I've got things to do.* I didn't have time to be sitting in school trying to burn up a frog that we were trying to dissect. And I didn't have time for a teacher who kept repeating the same thing over and over. So I would keep talking in class if the subject didn't interest me.

I always passed and I don't know how I fluked those results. I still have nightmares about exams. I probably shouldn't admit to this but on a multiple choice exam I'd ask myself, 'Which one is it: A, B, C, D or E?' and the answers would pop into my head and I'd pass. Not with ninety per cent or anything like that – but I'd get sixties and seventies without studying. I didn't like studying because it was boring; I had other things to do. I wanted to daydream about my life and where I wanted to go, and I liked hanging out with my next-door neighbours. The music industry course wasn't boring, though.

When it was over, we didn't see Ben, Chris or Dan again. That was it, and I was a bit saddened by it. I guess I'd grown used to them and Ben, in particular, was fun. But that was the end of that.

Before school was completely over we had the Year Twelve formal. I got all dressed up, of course, and as we sat in the hall I could see everyone looking beautiful. There were awards being handed out – and I should mention that the parents were there too. So my parents were there when I won something: 'The award for When Will I Be Famous? goes to Jackie Ivancevic.'

When I accepted my award I started by saying, 'I would like to thank God.' I gave the speech like I was at the Grammy Awards, standing there in my beaded bone-coloured dress, saying, 'I'd like to thank all my fans out there for voting for me to receive this.' They even gave me a certificate. Now, you'll remember that as a child I used to sign my cards 'Famous Jackie' – the award wasn't a surprise to me. In fact, I thought it was amazing. I always knew there was something more I was going to do; I couldn't put my finger on it but I knew it was something bigger than me – I wanted to do something for the greater good. (And, honestly, I don't think I'm there yet; I think I'm part of the way there.) My soul was reaching out and talking to me, and I was listening.

I can see now that by the end of school there was a reason for all the things that had happened to me: being European and singled out for it at school, going to that music industry course, and the way events were unfolding and putting things in front of me. Everything was preparing me for the next stages of my life and for the types of people I would be associating with. At the time I wasn't aware of it, but I can see now that it was part of a bigger plan: the universe was giving me all this preparation.

At the end of school I was seventeen. I asked myself the questions a lot of people do when they finish high school: *What am I going to do? Am I going to study? Should I go to university?* I thought, *I'm not going to study – who wants to go to university? Not me!* I didn't want to spend another five years studying. Besides, I was still young and figuring stuff out.

I was clear about something, though: I always knew that I wanted to be in the entertainment industry or I wanted to help people. Even when I was daydreaming I used to have this thing in my head that Oprah Winfrey inspired me, music inspired me, dance inspired me. I remember watching Oprah Winfrey from a very, very young age. And I remember when she had her big hair and the budget for her show wasn't high, because when I was watching her it was a very small studio and the set was bland. But it was never about her set – it was about the way she struck a chord inside me. I believe that

Oprah Winfrey channels when she talks, and I believe that she's done that her whole life and probably didn't even realise it at first.

What I didn't have were plans for how to help people. So I went to Croatia for a while, and when I returned I didn't know what my next step would be.

My aunty was working in a bank – she's not my real aunty, she's just called aunty because she's a very good friend of my parents. She lived in the Eastern Suburbs of Sydney and I used to visit her sometimes. She said to my parents, 'I can get Jackie a job in corporate banking.' By then I was eighteen, nearly nineteen, and I was naïve. I had not gone out pashing boys, I had not gone out partying. I was sheltered because my parents didn't want me to be around people doing drugs or anything like that, and I was a good girl who listened to her parents.

I got the job. Corporate banking is not like working in a branch where there are a few tellers. I wasn't a teller per se: there were only five people who would come into the bank with money from their business, and always large amounts.

My manager at the bank was a woman called Donna; I'm still in contact with her. My dad was working in Sydney so we shared a house in Lane Cove and Dad would go home to Newcastle on the weekends. One day he walked into the bank and said, 'Who's the manager here?' After he was introduced to Donna, he said, 'Jackie is a bit naïve, she's never lived outside Newcastle, and she's moving to Sydney for work. So she needs to be looked after.' My workplace wasn't dangerous but my dad didn't want me to know or get close to the people I was serving because I was young and some of the customers were European guys who went for girls like me.

Maybe Dad had an inkling about what sort of people I'd meet at the bank – that is, the sort who often arrived with bodyguards. I'd be there wondering, *Why is this man coming in with five bodyguards? Why is it that people are escorting him in? And why is it that he's seventy and he can hardly talk and he's Italian, and he has bags of money and he owns half of the nightclubs in Sydney?*

One client was a man who owned a few nightclubs, and he'd come in with his entourage. At the bank they could clearly see that I was this good European girl, and Donna knew what my dad had asked her to do, so when this client arrived she'd say, 'Jackie, go out the back – I'm going to serve these people.' She knew they'd try to ask me to go out with them. And I was so naïve for so long – right up until my relationship with Paul – that I would have gone.

There was this one good-looking guy who was around thirty-two. He'd always say, 'Hi Jackie, how are you? Do you want to go for a coffee? Would you like to go for dinner?'

Donna would bustle over, saying, 'No, she can't do that. Jackie, go to the back office, you've got to go and do some filing.'

'But he's good-looking,' I'd say. I wanted to go out with him but Donna didn't give me a chance to say yes.

Then she'd come back to where I was working and say, 'You are not going with any of these guys.' I'd ask her why and she'd say, 'They're not for you, Jackie. They're older, you're younger – you don't need a 32-year-old, you need somebody who's eighteen or nineteen.'

One of my colleagues, John, would also say, 'You don't need to hang out with those guys. Of course, you could, but don't worry about them.' When those clients arrived, if Donna didn't get in first, John would shove me over and say, 'Go and do some filing.' I used to think, *Why the hell am I always sent off to file?* I thought they were treating me like a kid, although now I realise I was being protected.

There were several opportunities presented to me while I worked at that bank – that is, chances to go out with different sorts of guys. I could have ended up with quite a different life if I'd followed one of those paths. Instead I think this was another way that I was shown lots of types of people – in this instance, colourful people – but I didn't judge any of them for what they did to earn a living, or for who they were in any aspect of their lives.

I might have been outspoken but I came from a very protected upbringing. When I was twelve, thirteen, fourteen years of age I'd go to bed at eight-thirty and when I got a bit older I was allowed to stay up to nine-thirty and ten-thirty. I could play on our pushbikes and we'd go to the shop and we'd go down to the lake – that was the extent of my adventures in my childhood. Even into my teenage years I wasn't trying to sneak out at night to go drinking or meet boys. I certainly didn't meet the sorts of people I met at the bank. Working there opened my eyes to new people, and prepared me to encounter lots of different people when I started working as a psychic.

I worked there for three and a half years and then I wanted to go overseas again. I took a year off and went back to Croatia. I loved it – I wanted to live there and I used to tell myself, 'I'm going to live six months of the year here and six months in Australia.' I knew that I would eventually have my own place there and I would live there because I love that country so much; there's such a connection for me. Everyone would say, 'Get your head out of the clouds.' But, just quietly, I now live part of every year in Croatia.

Once I came back to Australia I realised I never really liked working for other people and wanted to work for myself, even though I didn't know what I'd do and I couldn't do it right away. So I went from working in corporate banking to retail banking, and I worked casually. They would ring the office and say, 'Can you work this shift or that shift?' I loved it because there were times when I would say, 'No, I'm not working today – I'm going for a swim.' But they would always offer me work because I really hit the sales targets, being such a good talker. I won awards for my work.

I even lied a couple of times and said I couldn't work because there was something wrong with my throat, or I wasn't feeling well, and then I'd be over at the beach. I got caught out. There wasn't even a reason to lie because I could say no anyway – but I felt guilty for lying. I grew up with Croatian guilt: I would feel guilty if somebody asked me to do something and I said no, and then I'd feel guilty for letting them down. That's how I was raised. I'd never say no – if my dad told me to go and do something, I'd go and do it. There were no *nos* allowed. All my dad had to do was give me a look and I'd do whatever he asked.

I still have a lot of guilt; that's something I work on. And at the time it meant that I wouldn't tell my mum and dad that I was saying no to work – even at that age I was still worrying about them. I was in my early twenties, though, so I just wanted to hang out at the beach three days a week or go to the movies, sit around, drive around in my Capri. I'd just daydream, sitting at the beach, thinking, *This is my life and I love it.* But I always knew there was something more that I needed to be doing.

I was still thinking about this relationship I wanted – and the marriage that I wanted. I wanted to live overseas. I thought I'd love to just be at home and cook and clean, but I also still wanted to be known and to help people. It was a conundrum, wanting these things that seemed the opposite of each other.

It was at this time that I was in that relationship with Paul. After it was over, I wrote a list of qualities I wanted in a man and said to my angels, 'I'm not going to date anybody else until I have all these things.' I was swearing at God – and by the way I didn't start swearing until I was twenty-four. After years of not being allowed, one day it just all came out. I am sure it was the emotional fallout from that relationship that changed my behaviour – I wasn't going to be shackled in any way ever again.

So I wrote a list and I swore at the universe and I said, 'I've had my heart broken' – or what I thought was broken. Now I look at it, my heart wasn't truly broken, the pain was just me wanting control. I was so upset because I felt like I'd given my all to somebody who didn't deserve it, and I was angry about it. I didn't have the tools to manage what happens when you're in a relationship and how it changes over time. I just thought that everyone was kind to one another and you're nice to the other person and you give them respect. I had never experienced behaviour like that before, so I had no idea how to cope with it. I had no template for dealing with it. My dad never did that to me; he was controlling in the sense of telling me I had to cook and clean the house, but I was still able to go and play with the neighbours or speak out if I needed to. I wasn't locked in a house, he didn't tell me what to wear or anything like that. So what I experienced with Paul was completely different – and incredibly disempowering.

I didn't date anyone for a few years after the end of that relationship. At first I was just too shattered, but after a while I'd go out and have coffees but I wasn't dating, I wasn't sleeping with anyone, I wasn't kissing anybody, because I said, 'I will not and that's that.' By this stage I was in my mid-twenties; I was working as a psychic medium, and I focused on that. I also had my family, and I made sure I was doing things I enjoyed. There were times I'd get upset and I'd say to the universe, 'I'm ready for a relationship – what's taking so long? I want that man. Tell me how he looks, angels – show me how he looks.' When I yell at the universe I get over it, but the frustration was real. I'd keep asking, 'What does he look like?' I'd close my eyes and always see myself in a wedding dress, and I'd see the man in a black suit and I'd see a bit of longish hair – but I'd still never see his face. Sometimes I'd wish it was my ex – which seems ridiculous now because a few years had passed since we split up. I couldn't help what I was thinking and feeling, but I knew it wasn't him in my visions even though I couldn't see the man's face.

Then one day I had a phone call from Jane, a girl I hadn't seen in a few years. We were friends in Newcastle when I was younger but we were moving in different circles by then. She was calling to say she'd moved to Bondi.

'I'm having a housewarming party on Saturday,' she said, 'and I want you to come.'

Immediately I said, 'No, I don't want to come.' I thought I knew what sort of party it would be and I was staying away from toxic situations and environments. By this point I had made a name for myself in Newcastle as Jackie the psychic. When I went out with my friends, people would come up to talk to me – they'd stare at me. Some would be people I'd given readings to, and they would tell me how much I'd helped them, which made my heart sing. It also meant my life was very different from how it had been when I was friends with Jane, and I wasn't sure I wanted to reconnect with my old life.

On the Saturday evening, after my readings had finished, and although I wasn't really drinking much, I went to the bottle shop and got myself a bottle of red wine. I thought, *I'll just have a glass of red and I'll watch television, maybe a movie.* I had a couple of sips of the wine, then a message popped strongly into my head: *Get dressed*, I heard, *and go to that party.*

I countered with: *I don't want to go to that party!* But again there was something in my head that told me to get up, get dressed and go. So I thought, *All right, I'll get ready and drive down to Sydney*, which would take a couple of hours. Now I was thinking, *I feel like going out to dance.*

I rang a friend who lived in Sydney and said, 'I'm picking you up – you're coming with me to a party.' I knew that, like me, she wouldn't be out for a wild night.

When we arrived, Jane said, 'Jackie! How are you? What's going on?'

I said congratulations on her new place and handed over the drinks we'd brought with us.

All the cool kids of Bondi were there. There were all these surfers and some actors.

I hadn't managed to get very far into the party when in walked three guys and another guy behind them.

One of them said, 'Hey – Jackie!'

'I know you,' I said.

'I came from Sydney to get a reading from you,' the guy said, 'and you were spot on, man – you have no idea.' Then he turned to one of the other guys and said, 'Tom, you should get a reading from her.'

So this Tom said, 'What can you tell me?'

I started giving him messages, and his eyes widened more with each one.

As I was speaking, another guy walked through the group.

He looked at me and said, 'I know you.'

I hadn't recognised him straightaway but I started to work it out. I didn't say anything, though, I just walked away.

Then he called out: 'I remember your walk. You're Jackie from TAFE.'

I turned back and said, 'Oh, yeah – and you're Ben, I remember you too.' He looked very fit and he had this hat on, looking like a real rock star – well, he *is* a rock star.

'What are you doing here?' he said.

'I know Jane.'

'Yeah, I know Jane too. We're just stopping in.'

Ben had rented a place in Bondi. He was training every day and working on his music, getting prepared for the next Silverchair record. We kept talking and I could see that some of the girls at the party were getting a bit upset that I was speaking to him, although I didn't really think anything about it – we knew each other from years before, so it was two classmates catching up. But I also had other plans that night.

I said, 'My friend and I are going to the Ivy,' which is a nightclub in the city. 'I want to go and dance. Everyone here's getting wasted and I'm not interested.'

Ben said, 'I'm going there too – how about you give me a lift?'

That seemed like a reasonable request, so I drove us all into the city.

When we arrived at the Ivy we headed to the top level, where there was a pool bar. It was a popular spot for people to hang out. Ben had my girlfriend on one side and me on the other side, and we hooked our arms through his, like mates.

When we arrived at the pool bar he said, 'Can I have your number?'

'You're not getting my number, because I know what you want. You can have my psychic number, though.' I meant the number I used for work.

He was being cheeky, and he laughed at me.

'What are you doing here, anyway?' I said.

'I'm meeting up with a chick,' he said.

'Of course you've got to meet up with a girl, don't you?' I was laughing back at him, but that was because our past connection had been reawakened.

I saw the chick he was meeting up with – she was a Shirelle. I called all his girls Shirelles. Ben was seeing a number of girls, and he told me he was always clear about the relationships being short term and 'fun'. So, rather than learn all of their names, I called them all one name. She ran up to him and I thought, *What the hell is this girl doing?* She was carrying on in what I thought was a fairly strange way: she was giving me death stares while I was talking to Ben, and she wouldn't let him out of his sight. But I wasn't looking at Ben like he was famous: I was looking at him as a man, as a person.

I saw him for who he really was. But he had a date, and I had to leave them to it.

'Ta-ta,' I said, 'enjoy yourself.'

During the rest of the evening I could see them over the other side of the bar, drinking champagne, and he was leaning in to listen to her as she talked. By then he'd given me his number so I texted him a message: *That looks fun – not.*

He'd already told me that he didn't usually answer his phone straightaway, but I saw him pull it out and read the message. He looked over at me, then I turned away to talk to my friend. We decided to go. I didn't say goodbye to him – I just left.

I had a dream that night, and the next day I rang Ben and said, 'I had a dream about you.'

'I had a dream about you too,' he said.

We started describing our dreams. I dreamt I was going through a gate; there was a pool and he was standing on the other side of it. I just felt safe. I looked at him and I just knew – I had this feeling of being home, this safe feeling. He'd had the same dream, but in his, I was on the other side of the pool.

'This is weird,' he said.

For me it wasn't weird, but I did wonder, *Why am I dreaming of you? Am I dreaming this because I have to give you a message?* It was like I was being guided to see that this was someone who was going to be important to me. Water means emotion, and I felt like Ben could be my safe place.

Then he said, 'Can we meet up?'

I said no, but then he said, 'I want a reading.'

* * *

About three weeks later I rang Ben because I'd had another dream about him. He answered the call while he was with his bandmate Chris; they were working on their music. He talked to me for forty minutes, and I could hear somebody in the background saying, 'Gillies, what is taking you so long? Why are you still on the phone?'

He said to me, 'Look, I really want a psychic reading.'

I still wasn't sure about that, so I said, 'Let me think about it.'

That week I did my scheduled readings for other people, and by Saturday I thought, *I'm going to message Ben and say he can come over for a reading.* I thought I'd give him a reading because he kept saying how he really wanted to hear from his grandfather and how close they had been. I didn't have any romantic interest in him at this point – at all – and I was feeling drained after a big week, but I texted: *Hi, how are you? If you want to come to my place, come over and I'll give you a reading.*

He was on his way back to Newcastle so he said he'd stop in around seven or seven-thirty. When he arrived his whole face went pink – he got embarrassed, even though I know now that Ben doesn't get embarrassed. Of course, it was because he liked me, but I just didn't see it – well, I kind of saw it but didn't see it, if you know what I mean. I thought he just wanted a shag.

I looked at him and said, 'Come in – don't be embarrassed! What are you embarrassed about? Why is your face all pink?' Then I said, 'Your spirits are already here. Tez is here and Donald's here.' Don's his grandfather's name, which I didn't know at the time, and Tezza was his dad's best friend, who had died of cancer. I said, 'They're here and they're ready to speak to you.'

Ben started freaking out a little bit, but I began the reading. I don't remember what I said, but Ben has since told me. He said, 'You can't make that stuff up.' Even if he thought I had googled him, the names of his grandfather and his dad's best friend were not something I could have found.

I believe the spirit world was connecting Ben to me. And in the meantime I was acting as if I was in a loving, beautiful relationship because I was working on manifesting that kind of relationship.

After that night, Ben and I would always hang out, but he was still running around with other girls, so I was just his mate. As soon as I'd finish work I'd get onto Facebook and Ben would always be creeping around there. Every time I'd get online he'd be straight on too: *Hi Jacks, how's it going, love ya, when are you coming over, let's have a drink.* I'd write back: *Yeah, I'll come over.* Soon enough we were hanging out all the time.

We became best mates, and we hung out as best mates for a long time. We used to go on holidays together. We'd go to the Hunter Valley for day trips. He'd be invited to dinner parties and he'd always say, 'Jackie, come with me.'

There was one Christmas party I was invited to and he was there with a girl, but even when he was with other girls he'd always sit next to me and check on me. I'd say, 'Just go back to your girlfriends.' But I could see too that those girls were getting cut, because they knew he had no interest in them, he was interested in somebody else – and it was more than an interest. I was not just a shag to Ben – there was always more there. He really cared for me. But I'd go to his house and sometimes I'd sit in the car and think, *What am I doing here?* while he'd be at the door waiting for me to come up the stairs.

His house was right on the beach: you could sit out the front and look at the water. It was so beautiful, and I'd say to him, 'This is so nice, this place,' and he'd say, 'Yeah, it's all right.' He was so humble.

I didn't touch him the whole time we were hanging out. Sometimes we slept in the same bed, but I never, ever touched him. There were times he'd try to give me a kiss and I'd say, 'Don't touch me, Ben. For me to kiss somebody it has to mean something.'

There was one time he was really upset; he was sitting on the beach worrying about something, I think it was about life and women and people using him and all those sort of things. I said to him: 'You've got to snap out of it, mate! You're living a life that most human beings can't attain, that they will never experience. You're blessed! You have been given something that you should be giving thanks for every day.'

And Ben is a thankful person, but at that point in time he was more thinking about all the girls who had used him, his friends who had probably used him, people he'd been a very loyal friend to who had done the wrong thing by him and he was hurt by that.

I said, 'Do you know what love is? Love is when you know that person is there for you unconditionally and without judgement.'

He said, 'I don't know that – every chick I've been with has always been there for other reasons, not for me.'

What those girls wanted wasn't the person Ben is but the life they thought he could give them, and guys can see through that.

Ben had already been through that kind of thing, too; he was not going to go through it again. But I started to see girls getting upset whenever Ben would take me anywhere, because they liked him but he liked me. He'd even say, 'You know I like you, Jackie, why don't we just give it a go?'

I'd say, 'There's nothing to give a go, Ben. It's not going to happen, mate.' Because at that stage I still genuinely wasn't interested in him like that.

Then there was this one time we were at the beach and he was cracking onto another girl. I found myself feeling a little bit jealous. *What the hell am I jealous for*, I thought. Ben was drunk, he'd just pashed this girl and he'd probably shagged her too – God knows, I didn't ask him. It was easy for him to do that because there were always girls willing to be with him. On this occasion

I was jealous because I'd never seen him kiss a girl in front of me – he would always go away and I would never know about it.

I used to leave things at Ben's house: I had my swimming costume hanging up in his bathroom; I had my high heels on the floor because I'd go to his house to get ready to go out with him – we were besties. One girl he brought home said, 'Is this your girlfriend's stuff?' His answer was: 'Don't worry about it – that's Jackie's stuff.'

That time I saw him kissing another girl, though, was when I started to feel like I was interested in him after all. But I wasn't going to allow myself to go further when he wasn't ready for anything serious. I wasn't going to push it, and I wasn't going to be with a guy who only wanted to go out and shag chicks, because I'd decided I wasn't doing that.

One day we went to the vineyards and he said, 'When are you going to let me take you out for dinner?' because every time we'd go out we would go halves and he wasn't used to that. I'd always pay half; even if I didn't have much money I'd pay my way – I was doing my readings but still giving money to charity, so while I earned good money I didn't always have a lot of cash. No matter where we were, whatever was going on, that was my thing. If people were there and they weren't being very nice to me, I'd still buy them drinks.

Ben told me later that he was kind of testing me. All the time we hung out – about a year – he thought maybe I wasn't who I presented as. That was understandable, considering his past experiences. But I am *always* as you find me – what you see is what you get.

This time when he asked if he could take me out to dinner, I said, 'All right, you can take me out for dinner,' and Ben decided on a really nice fine dining restaurant in the vineyards.

At the dinner, he said, 'I'll order the champagne for us,' and I thought it was sexy. Then he said, 'I'm ordering our food, Jackie,' and I thought that was hot because I like a man who can take control – in a certain way. I don't like it when people are *controlling* – there's a difference. But I loved that he did that. It conveys the impression that you're confident about who you are. And Ben is very confident about who he is – not out of ego, but because he knows himself.

So he ordered dinner and we had the best time. At the end of the night, he tried to kiss me again.

'It's not going to happen, Ben,' I said.

He was still leaning in towards me.

I said, 'Get your face away, it's not going to happen.'

We went back to the house and we were lying in bed – staying in the same bed, as we often did. 'I want to tell you something,' he said, and I knew he was going to tell me he loved me.

I had this nervous feeling in my gut, so I said, 'No, you've got nothing to tell me.'

So he wrote it on a note and chucked it at me, then he ran into the bathroom. I thought that was really cute.

I looked at the note. It said, *I love you.*

When he came back, he said, 'Have you read that note?'

'No,' I said, 'I haven't.' I didn't want to acknowledge what was happening because I wasn't sure I'd know how to get myself out of the situation. I knew I was developing feelings for him but I absolutely did not want to end up in the same kind of relationship as I'd had before. I wouldn't allow myself to. And because that was the only relationship I'd really had, it was my point of comparison.

Ben wasn't giving up, though. 'Let's go to Bundeena,' he said. Bundeena is a beautiful beachside town in Sydney's Sutherland Shire. I had no objection to going, so I agreed.

'I'll pay for it,' he said.

'No, you're not paying for it, mate,' I said. 'We're going halves.' I might have let him take me to dinner but as far as I was concerned that was a one-off, because I believe that when someone else starts paying for you that means that they expect something they're not paying for, like a kiss.

So we went halves. When we got to Bundeena we were hanging out in this little shack on the beach. It was such a lovely setting, next to rocks and the water. I'd brought my music and I was dancing around in my swimming costume, having a wonderful time. We'd lie on the beach and talk about life.

Meanwhile, I was still having conversations with the universe about the relationship I wanted. I was saying, 'It can't be Ben I have a relationship with – come on, this is not who I'm going to end up with. Ben is not the tallest guy you'll ever meet and I wanted a tall European dude. He's quirky, and I'm into hip hop and R&B. This ain't going to happen!'

But as we were lying on the beach one night, I closed my eyes. My body was half in the water and half on the beach because it was such a hot night. We'd been out for a few drinks and I was tipsy. Ben leaned over and kissed me. And I kissed him back. And that's all we did.

When I woke up the next day I was so embarrassed. I didn't know what to do because he was still asleep. So I wrote him a note: *Now you've pashed me, and I told you I didn't want to kiss you but you kissed me anyway, so now you're going to have to marry me.*

I went outside and I sat there thinking, *What am I going to do? I've just kissed this dude, and I am so embarrassed I can't look at him now. He's my friend, and that's going to change.*

Then Ben came out of the house – a bit hungover – and he said, 'I read your note.'

I really had no idea what would happen next.

'So,' he continued, 'where's the priest? I'll marry you now.'

'What?' I said. 'No, you won't!'

He wouldn't let it go, and I was pretty sure he was making fun of the whole thing. A part of me got a little excited by it, though, so I said, 'We can go and find one.'

'Okay,' he said. 'Let's go find one, because I'll marry you.'

But I just said, 'Let's get some more vodka into me right now.' I couldn't quite believe what was happening.

That night Ben and I went out to the local pub. This other guy tried to crack onto me, and he put his arm around me. I grabbed him and said, 'Get your hand off me.'

And while that was going on, this chick appeared next to Ben, grabbed him and tried to kiss him.

My guts dropped. Not only that, she spilled her drink on my white shorts. I had half a mind to stand up and say something, but I decided against it.

Instead, I stood up and went to the bathroom, where I started getting a bit emotional. I got it under control, though, then said, 'Ben, I'm leaving,' and walked out. I didn't care if he wanted to stay; I knew how to get back to the shack and I really wanted to leave.

He followed me and said, 'What's wrong?'

'Nothing,' I said. But then I changed my mind and gave it to him.

I think he was quite taken aback, because I finished with, 'Anyway, our kiss meant nothing. I don't want you anyway.'

We arrived back at the shack, and by this time I was crying.

I said to the universe, 'Right – I pashed this dude. And I told you what I wanted. I didn't date anyone for years and now is the time! I will not go back and I will not do psychic readings. I'll be done with you and I'll be done with all this shit.'

Obviously, I was pretty upset to say something like that. But I had more.

I said, 'I've kissed this guy and now I've got strong feelings for him. I feel like I'm falling in love with him.' And this is not something I say lightly, let me tell you. 'You'd better show me now, not tomorrow, not in a week, not in a month, not in a year – you show me *now*.'

Meanwhile Ben's trying to talk to me, so I said to him, 'Get away from me because I don't want to see you – in fact, I'll sleep out here and I don't care that it's thirty-four degrees.' It was stinking hot that night, but I didn't want to be around him.

Ben knew all about Archangel Michael because I'd given him a necklace with Archangel Michael on it. So then – he told me later – he was crying and praying to Archangel Michael. He told me that even though he'd never prayed in his life, he didn't want to lose me. He said to Archangel Michael, 'I don't want to lose her. Please, please let her see how much I love her.'

I slept on the lounge, as I said I would. I was angry at him because I was supposed to be his friend, so even if I wasn't with him romantically he was supposed to protect our friendship and make sure I felt safe. That night I felt anything but safe with him.

During the night, while I was asleep, Ben got up. Outside the shack there were several frangipani trees. He got a plastic bag and filled it with frangipanis. Then he wrote several notes.

That night I dreamt about my ex, Paul. And I dreamt about Ben. That dream showed me everything I went through with Paul and what would have happened if I'd stayed with him, but I was also shown what was happening with Ben. There was a pool again, and French doors, and Paul was there. It was almost like he wanted me back, and then there was this part when they were both there. I also dreamt about a family member who had passed away and they had said to me about Ben, 'This man is the one – he is the one,' and I knew it was true.

But when I woke up I saw him sitting near me, and I gave him a filthy look. That's when I saw frangipanis spread all over me and the notes that said *I love you.*

I love you, I love you, I love you.

It was very hard to not believe him. But I didn't want to look at him.

'I love you too,' I said. And he kissed me and I forgave him.

The next day I rang my mother; she'd met Ben but Dad hadn't. I said, 'Mum, I dreamt that Ben's going to propose to me.'

She said, 'No, he's not.'

'He's proposing to me,' I insisted.

'Don't be so ridiculous,' she said.

Two days later Ben asked if we could go for a walk, and we ended up at waterfalls. We were sitting on the beach afterwards and Ben said, 'Come here.'

He got down on one knee and I started laughing. 'What are you doing?' I said.

He pulled out this ring that, to be honest, wasn't that impressive, and tried to put it on my finger.

'Will you marry me?' he said.

'What?' I said.

'Will you marry me?'

That time I said, 'Yes.'

It was an amazing moment – however, I started laughing again, and said, 'But can I please say something? Can we maybe go halves in a ring? Please – because this ring looks like it's worth maybe two hundred bucks.'

He started laughing then popped open the champagne. That's when he pulled out a small box and opened it. Now I was looking at a pink diamond – and I bawled my eyes out, because a pink diamond ring was what I'd always had on my vision board.

'I can't accept this,' I said.

'Yes, you can,' he said. 'You deserve it.'

I was crying, he was crying, we were hugging each other, and then I rang my dad and mum to tell them we were engaged – but little did I know that Ben had already rung my mother to tell her that he was going to propose, and he'd called her by the time I'd spoken to her a few days before. He'd also rung my dad and said, 'Ivan, I want to ask for Jackie's hand in marriage.'

The first thing Dad said was, 'Does she love you? Because if she doesn't love you then I'm not interested in you proposing to my daughter.'

I just couldn't believe I was engaged – it was all fairly surreal. I did love Ben, of course, which is why we got engaged and why we were married two months later without anybody knowing.

We went to the Registry Office and got married there, in the presence of my best friend, my sister and Goran, and Mum and Dad. Not even Ben's parents were there, because he didn't want anybody to know. Later we had a big wedding: church, celebrations, the whole thing. But nobody knew we were already married.

When I rocked up to the church there were about four cameras up a tree and another ten or so cameras at the gate. Apparently we were going to be on the news. I wasn't ready for any of that because I had never experienced it, so when I arrived at the church with Dad I looked out of the car and said, 'I don't want to get out.'

'Why?' Dad said. 'If you don't want to go inside, I'll keep going with you.'

I said, 'It's not that, Dad – look at those cameras up the tree. Can you not see that massive lens? Because I can and I don't want to get out!'

The priest who married us was so excited about being at our wedding that he allowed us to have alcohol in the church. He had somebody serving champagne and beers and shots and, as I'm sure you're aware, that's not the most common thing in the world. Our guests thought it was the best. At the reception we had a twenty-piece Brazilian band. It was an amazing wedding.

The angels always knew that I was going to marry Ben. Later he told me that he'd been too scared to ask me out, even when I was fifteen. He said, 'I liked you even then.' He'd even seen me once in a nightclub with a girl he didn't trust, so when he came up to say hello and saw her, he turned away. But I reckon that had to happen, because that's when Paul was in my life.

If I hadn't been through everything in the past, that moment in Bondi might not have happened. But we met again at the right moment. And I married my soulmate.

Not that everyone believes it. But I know that we love each other and allow each other to be who we are unconditionally.

I'll tell you what I think was an absolute blessing: that I was Ben's best friend for a year. I know the worst of the worst about Ben and I love him without judgement. And not many people can say that. I know every darkest secret about Ben, because when we were best friends we shared everything, we knew everything about one another. So we went into our relationship with no secrets – and even now, if he even thought about having a secret, I'd see it.

While I was praying for him he was praying for a girl like me. He's told me so. He was asking the universe for a girl who loved him for who he is and not the perception of who he is and what he may have. When I asked for my soulmate, I told the universe that I wanted somebody I knew everything about.

'You want me to teach other people,' I would say to the universe, 'you want me to show people that you can create your soulmate, that you can manifest that and that this actually really does exist but so many people think it doesn't.'

I used to think it didn't exist either, until I kept reading my books and meditating, and I thought, *My oath it exists, because that's what I deserve and if I don't have that I'll have myself to hug at night*. And Ben wanted the same thing.

I trust Ben completely. If he said he wanted to go away for six months, I couldn't stop him. I'd probably be cut for a second, but then I'd have to remember that I can't put conditions on any human being. I don't want conditions put on me so I cannot put conditions on him. If you're trying to put conditions on your partner, you're not loving them without judgement.

It's very hard to not be judgemental in a relationship – any relationship. Even with people in your family, people you've known your whole life, it's difficult, and there are a lot of family members who put judgements on each other. It's incredibly hard to not have judgements and it takes constant monitoring, but it's essential for a relationship to thrive. And that is what Ben and I have – a relationship that allows us both to shine and thrive.

* * *

Before I married Ben, my father used to call me a spinster. We'd go to other people's weddings – European weddings, that is – and people would ask him, 'Why isn't Jackie married? She's good-looking, she's got a good job, she's a good girl, she's so kind, she's confident, she's always hugging people, always making people feel nice and good about themselves.'

I was judged because I wasn't married and sometimes I'd think, *Maybe I am getting old. Maybe it's just not going to happen.* But then I'd come back to my faith: I *knew* it would happen and it would happen at the right time.

Having said that, I did feel a bit of pressure – but then I'd just snap out of it. I always preferred to be single than be in something like the relationship I'd left. I'd come this far in my spirituality and I was going to walk my talk. Certainly, there were times when I got angry, there were times I got frustrated, and I'd say, 'Where is he? *Where is he?* Is he ever coming?' There were times when I'd believe that I would be single for the rest of my life. But then I'd think, *No, actually, I'm going to find somebody and when I do find that somebody, it is going to be love that is true and real without conditions, without judgement, and someone who loves me for who I am.*

Ben loves me so much. He dotes on me. The things he does for me are incredible – and I do the same for him too. Actually, I don't think it's incredible. That's not the right word. I used to think it was incredible but what I've learnt is that every human being can have what we have. But it has to start with *you.* I've heard people say, 'I don't want to wait four years to meet someone,' and when I give readings, people don't like hearing that anything is going to take more than six months. Well, bad luck! Just because you still don't want to work on yourself, the right timing, the perfect timing, is the timing that is for the highest good, not when you want it.

That's what I was struggling with, though, before I met Ben. I wanted it *now*, not in ten years. Just because I'm aware of the tools that are needed to keep positive and work with the law of attraction doesn't mean that I still don't lose faith sometimes. I'd get frustrated. I have gone through all the emotions other people have felt in similar circumstances. But I know how to realign my thoughts to be positive. It's hard to stay positive, but once you learn how to stay committed in your mindset, it's much easier to do.

When love came to me, though, all those struggles were just gone. That's when I realised that keeping that faith and keeping that intention of acting as if I was in a loving relationship, and that I was happy, meant I started drawing that energy towards me. I put it out to the universe that I'd be married by the time I was thirty. At twenty-nine and a half I had no boyfriend and my father was saying, 'What's going on with you? You're nearly thirty. You're not seeing anybody.'

Not long after that, Ben proposed to me. We were married the day before my thirtieth birthday.

Real Housewife life

A year before I joined the cast of *The Real Housewives of Melbourne* I put something on my vision board: an image of six pairs of legs walking down a red carpet. You may remember my habit of writing 'Famous Jackie' on cards when I was a child; you may also remember that at my Year Twelve formal I was given the 'When Will I Be Famous?' award. And the only reason I was aware from a young age that I wanted to be known was that I knew I wanted to do great things in my life. I wanted to help people.

I remember watching the Grammys when CeCe Winans and Whitney Houston sang a gospel song and I started bawling my eyes out. I said, 'That's why I want to be known, Mum: to do what these people have just done to me. They've affected me.' I wanted to be able to affect people, so that they could have the life that they seek.

A year after I put that image on the vision board, I was watching *The Real Housewives of Beverly Hills* and I looked out at the beach, beyond our windows, and said to my husband, 'I'm going to be on a show like this.'

Ben laughed at me and said, 'Do you know how hard it is to get into TV?'

'Well, I'm going to be on a show like this,' I told him. 'It's going to happen.'

Within a few days I received a phone call from a friend; he had previously worked with the executive producer who was working on what was then called *The Real Housewives of Australia*. He was with the producer and called me to ask if I wanted to be put forward as a possible cast member. This friend said to me, 'What do you want to do?'

'Go for it,' I said.

He then told the producer about me and not long afterwards the producer called me. She asked if we were going to be in Melbourne.

I said, 'We're moving down to Melbourne.' We'd planned to, because Ben was looking for a creative change. The events synchronised themselves.

When I told Ben, he gave me this incredulous look and said, 'What the *hell*?'

'I told you I was going to be on that show,' I said.

At that stage the producers hadn't said yes to anybody because they were still going through the casting process, so they wanted to meet me in St Kilda with the casting producer, Katherine.

I flew to Melbourne for the meeting with Katherine and Lisa, the executive producer of the show, in a pub in St Kilda. Before I arrived my intuition told me, *You know that she's going to test you – this is why you're coming down. This is why she wants to meet you.* I even told Ben while we were on the plane that I thought she'd do that.

After we met and had a chat for while, Lisa said, 'What do you get from me?' She meant what kind of psychic vibes did I get from her.

I said something along the lines of, 'You've just broken up with your man. It was only a week ago.' I named him. 'And you've got two boys,' I added. 'Stop worrying about the kids and stop worrying about him. You're going to be fine financially and you're going to go and do your own thing.' I could see she was worried about her sons and worrying about how a change would affect all of them.

Then I said, 'Oh, and your grandfather is here. His name is Josef.'

'No, it's not,' she said, and she was quite adamant about it. But so was I.

'Yes, it is,' I said, 'because he's sitting behind you and telling me.'

'*No*,' she said.

I tried again. 'He's standing behind you and his name is Josef. Go and ring your mother, because he's here and she'll tell you that it's him.'

'His name is not Josef,' she said. 'It's David.'

But she got up and left the table to go to the bathroom. Without me knowing, she called her mother and asked what her grandfather's name was, and her mother said, 'David.'

'Is that the name he was born with?' Lisa asked. Her mother was a Holocaust survivor, and many Jewish people changed their names during World War II to avoid detection by the Nazis.

Her mother said, 'No, his real name is Josef.'

And Lisa started crying. She said, 'I'm here with Jackie the psychic, who I'm casting for *The Real Housewives of Melbourne*. You have never told me that my grandfather's real name was Josef.'

Her mother said he changed his name when he fled the camp, so he couldn't be tracked down.

Lisa came out of the bathroom and told me what her mother had said. 'How the hell did you know that?'

'Because I'm psychic,' I said.

Lisa turned to Katherine and said, 'This girl is the real deal. There's no way she could have known that about my family. *I* didn't know that.'

I knew the spirits were helping me, though – because they knew I would be tested. I was meant to be on that show and they helped put me there.

At that point I already knew I was in, and not just because of what happened when I met Lisa: I already knew that I was going to be on the show because I had manifested it. That didn't mean it was all straightforward, sign the contract, on we go. I needed some reassurances. So I said to the universe, 'If I'm to do this show, you'd better protect me, because I am not going on a show where I'm going to be smashed for what I believe in.' Because there are plenty of people who have adverse things to say about psychics and I understand that not everyone believes. 'All I ask is for some support so that I'm not made to look ridiculous.'

Before I signed the contract I said to the universe, 'Where is this going?' I meditated on it and saw that the show was going to be on prime time in the US, there would be several seasons and I would be on it. *There will be a few people who don't want you on it*, I heard, *but you are going to be on it and you are going to inspire people and you are going to help people. You've just got to stay true to who you are. Just be yourself.*

And I always have. I will say, too, that I'm very lucky to have Ben. He has supported me and because he has experience being in the public eye, he showed me what it would be like once I was on television. He warned me that there might be people saying stupid things about me and making up stories, and being horrible. Luckily, I don't read what people say about me. In the beginning I did fire back a few times, but then my spirituality kicked in and that's when I would pray and meditate on it. Luckily, the majority of my engagement with people online is incredibly positive, and I am grateful for that.

Before the show aired for the first time, I found myself speaking to Brian Walsh, the head honcho at Foxtel. He asked me how I thought the show would go, and I told him, 'Our show is going to America and it will go prime time and I'll meet Andy Cohen.' He said that wasn't going to happen because it had never happened before.

But I knew that our show was going to be a hit, although I also knew that some people weren't going to like the format and they'd think, *Why would you do a show like that? It's bitchy.* But I knew the show would give me an insight into other people, and help prepare me for my next step. There are always going to be haters, people on social media saying all sorts of rubbish, and I had to get prepared for what it's like to be in the public eye.

If you've watched *The Real Housewives of Melbourne*, you'll have seen that it was clear that Ben and I don't give a toss about what you have or don't have. What's really interesting, though, is to see how some people will only hang out with others if they have a certain status, or they meet certain criteria. That's not a judgement, just an observation.

After we moved to Melbourne, often the first question I was asked was, 'What school did you go to?' I went to a public school! Next!

What's really interesting is how people measure others by status and what they have and don't have, and what school they went to. But a lot of the time those are the people who don't have happiness. I don't care if you've got two bucks in your bank account. Is that really what life is about? Are you really happy or is it all a façade? And most of the time, with those people, it is a big façade.

Going on *Housewives* was good training to deal with people who are not happy with themselves. I just want to say, *Be nice to people and just be happy for people's success.*

Just before *Housewives* went to air I wrote to a couple of people at Foxtel and told them that it would go prime time in the US because I had dreamt it again. When they announced it, they hadn't told anyone in the cast, so you can imagine that there were people wondering how I knew. Maybe they thought someone had told me, but they hadn't: I knew a long time before. It was part of my reason for signing on: I did it because by going prime time, I knew that I'd be able to bring more awareness to what I do and therefore help more people.

The show has gone further than Australia and the US, too. I did go to America and appear on Andy Cohen's show; Andy is the executive producer of the American *Housewives* shows and has his own evening talk show. I'd already dreamt about being in Times Square with him, before I signed on and three years before it actually happened.

When I first went on Andy's show, I was alone, without any of the other Housewives. I went to New York City and did some promos and what have you. I was sitting there with him and I said, 'You've got a problem with your kneecap, you're going for an operation, and you're building a house in the Hamptons.'

Well, he couldn't believe what I'd said – because I was right.

He must have liked what he heard the first time because I was invited back again; he specifically asked for me and two other people to go.

The publicist said to me, 'Jackie, please don't give Andy any vibes.'

'What are you talking about?' I said. I couldn't believe that Andy had been upset about what I said the last time I was there.

'He was really rattled by what you told him,' the publicist said.

I found all of this a bit strange – he was so rattled by me that he invited me back? And not only that, he'd put me in his book. I clearly made an impression.

There was another aspect of that trip to America that made it seem surreal, even though I knew I'd manifested it. I always had a vibe that I'd be on the US *Today* show and, sure enough, I found myself sitting on the set with Hoda Kotb and two other Housewives while all these people were running around trying to take photos of us. And our faces were up in Times Square.

Now, this is a moment, I thought. Then: *Let's get on to the next thing.*

Becoming known was never about my ego. It was never because I thought I deserved to be famous. I always wanted to be well known so I could affect people on a much bigger scale. When you have a presence in the public eye, you're able to do things on a larger scale, and connect with more people. You can make a difference. For me, becoming better known was about increasing awareness of intuition and everyone's innate psychic abilities.

Even though some may see *The Real Housewives of Melbourne* as having a negative format, I don't look at anything as negative: even when things piss me off, I look at them as a blessing and I wonder what I'm able to take from it. When people write to me and say, 'You inspire me, you encapsulate such positivity,' I always say, 'It's not easy – you just need to keep your mindset there.' I am a very positive person and if something is negative I might dwell on it for a short time, and then I'll snap out of it.

If anything gave me an education in dealing with being in the public eye, being myself in front of a camera and dealing with confrontation on camera, and with trolls, it was being on *Housewives*. I reckon I'm better prepared than some of the actors who have been doing this stuff for twenty years. We Housewives can get instantaneously attacked about things. Now people could say the worst things about me and I'm at a point where I can handle it so well, it does not affect me. It's all in service of my higher purpose, and my next step, whatever that will be. I wasn't given any time to get used to fame. There was no time to wait around, this thing was happening *now*; there were going to be lovers, there were going to be haters, and I didn't have time to try to figure it out because it all happened so fast. It was reality TV.

What I found very, very hard about being on reality TV was that I was always authentic and true to who I am as a person, but not everyone else was. If you're not authentic you'll always be caught out; if you're not authentic the public will know. The viewers can see right through that bullshit, unless you're consistent – but it will eventually come out. Maybe my authenticity makes people sometimes think I'm full-on, and let me tell you – I know! I mean, if I met me, I'd think I'm full-on too, trust me on that!

Part of being true to myself is that I'm a very loyal person. So if you're my friend – and you can see this in the show – I will always stick up for you, but if my friends are in the wrong I'm going to call them out. Because I'm a genuine person and I have genuine friendships, I found it hard when there was a bit of wishy-washy, manipulative behaviour going on sometimes within the environment of the show. It might have been necessary for the storylines but it wasn't something I was comfortable with.

I always had to keep that higher purpose in mind. I knew that if I was going to do a show like this, people were going to watch, and I wanted to be able to inspire them. The only way to inspire is to be authentic. And the camera will always catch you out if you're lying. The camera has never caught me out, not once in five years, because I've never lied.

I think that people are drawn to those who are authentic; in general I believe that like attracts like. The people who like watching me on the show have always been very kind and supportive. If somebody else on the show said anything negative about me, I noticed that the people who follow me will stick up for me, but without being malicious. I believe I've attracted that energy and I like that I've attracted that energy.

I've always felt protected during the filming of the show. In my mind's eye I would see storylines before I even went into the season, and the producers wanted to know how I knew about them. I told them that the universe was protecting me.

I've had some interesting experiences with viewers, too. I might be sitting at the airport getting myself a little beverage while I'm waiting around, as you do, and some guy will come up and say, 'My wife loves you so much! She watches the show but she's not here.'

I'll say, 'Hang on, you watch the show too, dude.'

They usually say, 'All right, I do and I love it.' And I love it because if I can make somebody laugh then I know I'm doing my job, and if I can inspire somebody, I know I'm doing my job. People know I'm being myself on the show: my eyes and my facial expressions reveal how I'm really feeling. Viewers tell me that it's so refreshing to see someone who's so genuine on television.

You may remember one moment from season three when another cast member said to me, 'Oh, you're just from Newcastle,' and I was thinking, *Oh, please, you went to a state school too*. She said, 'You're from Newcastle and you don't know anything.'

Then I said, 'You know where you came from? Your mother's *pička*!' *Pička* means 'vagina' in Croatian. And by that I meant that we're all on the same level. I was angry with her, don't get me wrong, but what I really wanted to say was that no one's better than anyone else. So you know there are moments where I will lose my cool, and then I will centre myself and I will apologise if

I'm rude to somebody. I am a very passionate and feisty person, so even though I know my inner self and I know how to connect with that, there are still situations where I will lose my temper.

There was another time on the show when someone made me angry and, let's say, I got a bit passionate and feisty on camera. I felt as though I was let down. The drama is all part of the show, but that is how I felt in the moment.

When I saw myself on camera, I thought maybe I shouldn't have said what I said – but then I'm not going to regret what I said because that's how I felt.

There are times when we're filming that things would become very heated but the thing is: if any of these women rang me up at two o'clock in the morning needing help, I would go and pick them up. That's the person I am, that's the way I was raised.

Overall, while I don't love the arguments, I do enjoy doing the show. People don't want to sit around and watch us drink cups of tea, though, do they?

Boundaries and rebalancing

Being on *The Real Housewives of Melbourne* has brought me a level of fame – not that I'm fond of that word, but there aren't a lot of alternatives.

Ben has been famous for so long that it's like it's all he's ever known. For me, it's not. But I was able to deal with fame when it arrived because of *Housewives* thanks to having a super-humble husband who has achieved world recognition, twenty-one ARIA Awards – more than any other band in Australia – and so many other honours, and Ben is so humble. I come from a family that is humble and I also have a husband who is humble and says, 'Don't get caught up in hype, because you'll get swallowed up by it.' A lot of people do get caught up in the ego of it all. It can overinflate their image of themselves. It all depends on the intention: if you want to be famous for the sake of it, that sets you up for failure.

Initially I was uncomfortable about people recognising me, and I used to get a bit of social anxiety whenever I would go out. There were times when I didn't want to leave the house after the show started. That's the consequence of not growing up with strangers knowing who you are, as Ben did. Ben had fame instantaneously – and it really was crazy, what happened to that band – but he had two best friends he went around the world with and it was a different environment to the one I found myself in. People weren't bitching at him and screaming and carrying on! (But I do love the Housewives, really.) If it wasn't for Ben, I don't know how I would have coped. Possibly I would have got caught up in the ego, despite everything I've been practising all my life. I doubt it, though, because I knew who I was even before I met Ben.

But in saying that, I'm lucky the universe brought Ben into my life for so many reasons, including the support and help he's given me. My angels knew that I was going to keep progressing and this is where I'm creating and this is the space I'm creating, but I needed somebody to help me through it. Ben helped me through it. He said, 'Do not read anything,' about myself online or offline. So I don't. 'Once you start getting involved and reading things,' he told me, 'it starts to get into your head.' And you start processing the negative stuff over and over. Despite knowing that, though, I've done it: you can have a million positive comments and then you get to that one negative comment and you zoom in on it. Then I'll talk about it and repeat it to myself. But I have the tools to process it and I let it go.

The other thing I'm not comfortable with is that I don't like people staring. If we're in a restaurant and I can feel people staring, I start to think, *Is something wrong with me? Is that why they're staring?* And I won't enjoy myself. I'm still getting used to being recognised by people I don't know. I'm not sure if I ever will get used to it.

What can also happen is that because people see me on the show they think they completely know me, so they'll start telling me their problems – and that's okay, I can handle that, but if I'm out with Ben, it's my time with him and we need that. There have to be healthy boundaries. It has all been a big learning curve, but thanks to Ben, my family and my angels I have coped with the huge changes in my life. It is all what I have manifested and I feel blessed, and it's all part of my bigger life purpose to help people on a massive scale.

Then, in 2018 I had the opportunity to join the cast of the TV show *I'm a Celebrity ... Get Me Out of Here!*

I thought about it carefully and decided it would be an interesting experience, and it would give me the chance to raise money for the extraordinary Moira Kelly and her foundation, which was the cause I chose to support.

Moira is a woman making a huge difference in the world. She is a humanitarian who at eighteen worked alongside Mother Teresa in Calcutta. She is best known for helping bring conjoined twins Krishna and Trishna to Australia for the surgery that saved their lives. Her charity supports sick and needy children, their families and women who are struggling. She is one of my heroes and using my time in the jungle to support her charity felt right.

Before I went into the jungle I was staying in this beautiful resort – I had my own cook and everything; of course they were going to feed us up because they were about to send us into the jungle to survive on rations! I was enjoying myself because I knew that I wasn't going to be eating much in the camp and I am a massive eater. Funnily enough, before the show Ben and I had plans to prep me for it: training at the gym, no sugar, no alcohol, no coffee, and small portions of food. That all went out the window once I got to the resort!

Being in the jungle – and undergoing some of the tests and trials in that show – was an intense experience. I had plenty of time to think, and some of those thoughts were confronting. I realised I was impatient about some things that hadn't happened in my life. When I returned to Australia I had my Shine It Up tour to do, in front of audiences all over the country, then Ben and I went to Croatia for a while. But I still felt like I was asking for things to happen and they weren't happening quickly enough for me, and I was getting angry about that.

When I meditated on it, I was told that I'd lost my patience. Sometimes the universe will put things in front of me to make me stop. As I've always said, 'If I ever go off my path, you do something that's so drastic it puts me back on it.' Going into the jungle felt drastic. It made me realise not that I was going off my path but more that I was probably not giving myself the time I needed to balance all the energy that was going out, and that could have caused a burnout.

That experience in the jungle was a defining moment for me. It showed me that I'm still evolving – always evolving – and that I still have stuff I need to work on. And, more than that, I need to slow down. I had no idea, obviously, that it would turn out that way but I was glad it did. We all need reminders to get back on the path – to get back to ourselves – and that was mine.

Giving back

As you've probably picked up, giving back to others is very important to me. It was the main reason I did *I'm a Celebrity* – to raise awareness of the work of Moira Kelly's Creating Hope Foundation, and if I'd won, I would have raised more money for her.

I didn't start giving to charity because of any one person who asked me for money; my mother has said I was always giving money away. If somebody needed something I'd always be there to give it to them. Mum said that's how I was from a very young age. But it's hard to feel charitable when you're trying to pay a bill and you don't have the money – that's when you get frustrated and you get angry, and you're trying to have faith that abundance is coming to you, but that bill is due tomorrow.

In order to have more money so I could give to others, I had to learn how to remove myself from that kind of thought pattern. I had to not be focused on the bill that was due tomorrow and instead think about the money that was coming, and think of it as already being in my bank account.

However, charity isn't only about the money you can give. I went to a club one day years ago and there was this guy who had probably popped too many pills. He was lying on the ground outside the club, rolling around, and people were laughing at him. I didn't go out much at night because it was while I was working a lot as a psychic medium in Newcastle and I didn't want to go out and drink. But this night I felt like dancing and I went out with a couple of girlfriends.

I rang my friend Maria and I said, 'There's this guy here – I need to get him home. Nobody is helping him.'

Maria came to help me and we got him into the car. He said he lived in Toronto, which was a thirty-minute drive from this nightclub in Newcastle. He started saying, 'My mother's a slut, my dad does marijuana.'

I said, 'Yeah, yeah, it's all right, your mum might be a slut but you're in the car and you're safe.' I didn't know if he would get aggressive so I wanted to appease him.

Then I asked for his wallet as I also wanted to get his address from his driver's licence, if he had one.

I found his ID and rang his dad, and meanwhile this kid was starting to have a breakdown in the back of the car. I had no idea what he'd taken, and his friends had left him there even though he could have ended up in a very bad way.

This might sound like an extreme thing to do for a stranger, but all I knew was that it was my responsibility to help this guy, just like it's all of our responsibilities to help others. If I hadn't helped him when no one else would, what would have happened to him?

The good news for all of us is that you can help others by giving to charity – whether that's donating money or clothes or other items, or giving your time or helping someone in need – and that's the universe's way of telling you to keep your faith. When it comes to charity I believe that you need to give back and you need to help people, because that's what we're all here to do. If you can afford it you should be doing it, even if you can only afford to give two dollars away, or you could always donate your time – work a few hours at a soup kitchen, or a charity shop, or on a helpline. As I said, charity doesn't have to be about money.

Charity is important to me because I feel like it's the circle of life: if you've created abundance, you've got to do it for good, not just for yourself but for other people as well.

There were times when I gave money and my accountant told me that I really should not be giving anything. I always said it doesn't matter: money comes and goes. Money is an energy. It's an energy of receiving – giving it out, receiving it back.

In the past I wasn't very good at receiving emotionally, spiritually and physically, so I had to learn quickly that when I don't receive I cause a blockage within my own abundant manifestation. So if I'm going to give, give, give and somebody wants to give to me and I say no, then I'm not going to receive abundance because I'm stopping the flow. So then I started to learn to receive and give thanks, and positive energy increased around all aspects of my life.

* * *

Moira Kelly became my focus for *I'm a Celebrity* because she's a very special human being and the work she does is extraordinary.

I met Moira because of Chyka, who used to be on the *Housewives*. Chyka held an event to support Moira. We gave a donation, Chyka set up this beautiful lunch and we all got dressed up; media were there too. And that's where I met Moira – and she spoke some Croatian to me.

Moira had visited Bosnia during the Yugoslavian War. While she was there she helped children who had suffered because of the war, either through disease or injury. Some of them were maimed by bombings and they needed emergency care. But that's Moira's work: she goes all around the world and she takes kids from orphanages or kids who really need some medical treatment and brings them back to Australia. She gets them that treatment. She lives solely off donations.

I knew that I needed to do something for Moira because the things she does for children are amazing. It takes a special someone to do the work she does. The lengths she goes to so she can help kids are unbelievable. She works with severely disabled children, and children with really serious medical problems. One of the children has elephantiasis and that requires a lot of daily care. Another child has harlequin ichthyosis, which is a condition that affects the skin and makes it thick and hard.

The woman is tired – she's not going to admit it but she's tired – she hasn't had a break and she's forever working for those kids, and that's what she dedicates her life to. Someone else who worked on *Housewives* also became involved with Moira's work. She would take a couple of Moira's girls to her house once a fortnight to give Moira a break – she has so many kids and she rarely gets time off.

Years ago Mother Teresa gave Moira a medallion blessed by her. Before I went into the jungle she gave me that medallion, saying, 'If someone paid me a million dollars I would not do that. There's no way. I don't care what people think about me, I am not eating reptile eggs – no way in the world!' She knew it was something that was beyond my comfort zone but I wanted to do it to help her: this is a woman who is helping sick kids in developing countries that don't have the facilities we have here in Australia.

I think you've got to have a commitment and you've got to help these people. When I was in that jungle I would sit there and think, *Snap out of it! It doesn't matter that you're not seeing your husband. There are kids who are dying, kids who are in severe pain every day. You've got your legs, you've got your arms, and you have a good life. So snap out of it, Jackie, and get moving!*

If I wanted to cry I'd walk into the toilet and make sure that nobody saw me cry because I knew Moira's kids were watching the show and I didn't know what the cameras would capture. But just knowing those kids were watching every day motivated me. I would have loved to win *I'm A Celebrity … Get Me Out of Here!* because I felt a hundred thousand dollars would have been a huge help for Moira, and gain some publicity for her work. Regardless, it's an honour to know her and be able to support her and the children. Moira inspires me daily.

Shine it up

By now it should be clear to you that I am not the sort of person who comes to mind when you think of a psychic medium. I'm not a hippie chick. I go out. I drink. I dance. I swear. I'm an Aussie. I'm Croatian. But being a psychic and helping people is my life's purpose and the truth is everyone has one: you just need to tap into what your gifts are and use those for the good of other people. I have been able to dedicate myself to my life's purpose for over fourteen years and that's a blessing. But it's also something I have worked hard to create. I have had to be honest with myself and push myself at times to follow the right path.

There are many wonderful things in my life: my husband, my family, my friends, my work, the places I get to see and the opportunities I have. While some of these things – like my family – were handed to me, maintaining relationships with all the people I love is not something I take for granted. The life I have today is the result of me being dedicated to creating it. It all starts with a dedication to living a life that is emotionally, physically and spiritually authentic. I *want* to have good relationships with my loved ones: that's authentic to me. I *want* to help people through my work: that's authentic to me. I *want* abundance so I can give back to others: that's authentic to me.

Being authentic to yourself is important so you can live your best life possible. That means knowing that whatever it is that you're doing can have consequences if you're not living your authentic life. Be mindful of all your choices and actions.

If anything, I hope my story shows you that you should be living a life that is authentic *to you* – not what someone else thinks is authentic. Your thoughts create your experience on all levels, so if you are not being genuine with yourself, you are not creating the life you want. By doing something that's not right or true to you, you will create a consequence; it's likely going to create a negative impact within you and on your surroundings. So learn to make decisions that create positive impacts.

I learned the hard way that you can't manufacture a good life by lying to yourself. I was in a relationship that was emotionally draining. I had listened to my parents, I had listened to my teachers, I did everything the right way – I was a good girl. If my dad said, 'You're not going there,' I didn't go. But I went with this man who I thought loved me and I was going to marry him. I forgot about my spirituality. And that was being inauthentic. I had to wake up to the notion that knowing my self-worth is not about being egotistical, it's about doing better for myself and for other people. That's why I keep creating good intent, because I know that I do give a lot to people.

I know there are jealous people out there. Whenever someone is happy in their life, someone else is jealous of that happiness because of issues within themselves. They think they should have your happiness. Instead, they should look to their own. I bless those people with love and light. And I want to say to them, instead of being jealous, get inspired and do something positive for yourself.

There is no such thing as a perfect life. If I have a good life it's because I'm truthful to myself, whether it's negative or positive. There are a lot of people who aren't being honest with themselves. They think it's easier to have a façade. It's not.

People struggle because their idea of happiness is having their life be the way *they* see it – but that's not necessarily what's for the highest good. You can create the things you want in life but you can also spend a lot of time worrying about trying to control that process. Instead, trust that the universe has your back – the universe wants to give you what you ask for. But the biggest detriment to you is worrying and stressing about things; that creates a blockage. Having things is not going to make you happy unless you've already started working on yourself, and so many people don't want to work on themselves. They're looking outside themselves for that perfect relationship and eventually it catches up with them. Even if they think they have the perfect relationship for two years, three years, it catches up with them because what they realise is that their soul is yearning for something more; their soul is yearning for them to be truthful with themselves. They think they have the perfect relationship because it ticks imaginary boxes, but deep down they want something more meaningful and truthful.

As hard as it can be sometimes, I am truthful with myself, and I'm also true to who I am. As I've said, I'm not perfect. I have created a blessed life but that doesn't mean there aren't bad days, and bad times. I don't ever lose sight of who I am, though, and out of all the pain of the past, that is perhaps my greatest achievement: I emerged with a clear sense of who I am, and of what I can do. With that, I can set my intentions and make them happen. It is a constant practice, as I've said, but that's life: we don't get to clock out from being human.

I'm not special: you can create your life just as I have. I've shared my story because I want to encourage everyone to live their best life. We all have challenges. You may still have them. That doesn't mean your distress and pain are permanent. It doesn't mean you can't ever shine it up. If anything, it means you should dedicate yourself to shining it up *more*. Even in my very dark days, I was still talking about shining it up: *shine, shine, shine* showed me the path to the future I wanted. The future I set about creating.

I hope you will shine in your life: today, tomorrow, every day into the future. We all have a purpose; we all have talents and abilities. If you don't know yours yet, trust that you will. And don't be afraid to ask the universe for help, because it's there to support you. I don't do anything alone: I ask for help all the time.

Today's your day to shine it up. So get to it!

Acknowledgements

I want to start by saying a huge thank you to my little brother, Milan. He doesn't get as much page time within this book as my sister and other brother, but he is a very important part of our family! I love him so much. You'll always be my little snookles, Milly. Love you.

A huge thank you to Ben, Mum, Dad, Bobby, Angela, Kane, Gozzi, Eli, David, Kristy and Maria.

There are so many people who have been part of my journey. The book would need endless pages to name everyone!

Lastly, thank you to Sophie and everyone in the Hachette team. You've all made my first experience in the publishing world incredibly rewarding and fun. You've made my dream come true.